Dedicated

To the past, present and future lives of women.

&

To men striving for the lightness of being

The Problem With Women Is Men

Ron Seaborn

Life Line Inc., New York City

ISBN: 0-9647089-1-4

The Problem With Women Is Men

Printed in the United States of America.

Library of Congress Control Number: 2009903382

ISBN: 0-9647089-1-4

Visit our website: www.theproblemwithwomen.net

Acknowledgement

Kojo Ade
Jahari Adjiri
Audrye Arbee
Curtis Batts III
Dr. Delbert Blair
Angela Cola
Anthony Cola
Bara Cola
Richard Coleman
Lorna Cope
Brother Joseph Cox
Dr. Gerald Deas
Michele Dunbar
Beverly Flowers
Brad Gibson
Lonnie Gordon
Shilah Hill
Safeer Hopton
Deborah Johnson

David Johnson
Preston Johnson
Donald Jordon
Wendy Kilborn
Brett Linton
Maimuna
Kanya Vashon McGhee
Debra Naranjo
Diana Pharr
Albert Pierce
Jerry Pinks
Pauline Rogers
Winston Sanders
Dr. Sebi
Count Paul Stoval
Ronal Thomas
Bridget Walker
Sheryl Walker
Ted Wilson
Panzegna Wood

Editors: Louis Rivera
             Rachil Clark
*Special thanks to Gia Pampellone whose
computer knowledge was so necessary for the
life of this book, Daisy Lawrence and Dr. Padu
whose faith are unconditional.

Table of Contents

Foreword

This book reaches far and wide, casting a net around seemingly disparate concepts and bringing them to the table. What do sports, business, war and earth pollution have to do with romance? Ron Seaborn has created what can be called an "embracing" book about relationships: men to women, women to men, adults to children, all of us to the planet, and each of us to our spiritual selves.

It is a profound and thought-provoking book that you hold in your hands, a book that will give rise to much self-evaluation and reevaluation of events from your past as well as creating hope for the future of your relationships. Author Seaborn is wonderfully successful in stimulating intense awareness of our actions, motivations and habits and helps us to see the external connections that impact the internal emotions.

You'll wish that you had read this book a long time ago, had it been written. And you'll wish that you had read it before you started or ended that last relationship.

This book can give you a new perspective about what you bring to your relationships and how to look at your relationships, through the eyes of both practicality and spirituality. You may even find yourself committing to making personal change as a result of the wisdom found in these pages.

Ron Seaborn brings together so many diverse factors affecting relationships, tying one to another with extreme clarity. Every chapter is worth pondering, every major concept is show-stopping.

Read every sentence in this book.

Liah Kraft-Kristaine, J.D.

Author of twelve books, including the best-selling *"30 Days to Happiness"* and *"A Course in Becoming"*, Liah is a former practicing attorney, CNN television broadcaster and Hollywood television scriptwriter.

Introduction

There is a school of thought that states millions of years ago women and men were once one being. The theory states that through the process of evolution this one being separated to become female and male in order to help each other learn to appreciate the oneness in everything. If this is true, it illustrates how closely the lives of women and men were originally meant to be. Even though women and men are now separate individuals, when they unite as a couple they are and should be, in body, mind and spirit, one being.

In this book, I touch on the many challenges and issues that help to keep relationships off balance. The complexity of the challenges is made worse because the issues overlap each other and have existed throughout time.

The basic information we need and that most of us already know has been largely forgotten or taken for granted. There is nothing new being stated here. It's all been said and done before. However, I am presenting the information in a way that might help us to apply it to today's situations more effectively.

All of the chapters here have some bearing on our interaction with each other, especially the metaphysical chapters. We are not just physical beings. We are also spiritual beings, including those who have committed the most heinous crimes; they just have a greater lesson to learn. Therefore, a metaphysical understanding of each other can have a profound effect on our mental and spiritual growth. The growth of our minds and spirits builds a foundation that enables us to become better humans and will automatically result in better relationships in a better world.

Many of us approach life with polarity consciousness believing that everything is separate and not connected. However, nothing is separate. Everything is connected. It's like a domino effect – any one thing affects everything.

There is a book called The Kybalion, which contains the knowledge of Thoth, better known to the Western World as Hermes Trismegistus. His contemporaries considered Hermes a God, and all the greatest minds of antiquity came to sit at his feet to listen to his wisdom. The Kybalion was written by three initiates who wanted to pass Hermes' teachings to the world without personally taking credit for the profound knowledge they had obtained. The Kybalion is written in a way that leaves the reader motivated to read more books on the subject. Similarly, all of the chapters in this book could be expanded into a series of separate books. However, my intent is to create basic awareness that could also motivate the reader to do more research in obtaining information that will lead to peace of mind, love and knowledge.

The Problem with Women
Is Men

Ron Seaborn

Out of New Rock

Men

Why is there a problem with woman, and why has the problem been so difficult to solve? Men have shaped the world to suit themselves without considering women, and women have reacted against this lack of consideration.

The initial thought that man had regarding women led to women being treated as inferiors. How could man be made in the image of God and woman made from a man's rib? All life comes through the female of every species. Was man so insecure that he purposely misrepresented the facts? Were the insecurities so great that he chose to polarize himself from his other half?

The price that we have paid for accepting this misinformation should demonstrate to modern man that

1

we are still on the path of pain. In order to effectively move away from this misguided approach we need to balance ourselves.

Man cannot succeed in a holistic world using only half of self. In order to balance our environment and ourselves, men must accept women as equals so that we can function as a whole.

Men must stop and think. Most of us do not think about our actions or the consequences. Many of us act impulsively out of fear or out of a selfish desire to obtain our goals, and this is how we create problems that block our blessings. Why not think about our goals and discuss them with others or voice them out loud to ourselves before acting? This approach can help to stop us from acting selfishly.

One of our goals should be to establish the balance that will achieve joy in life for all, a win-win situation. Even though polarity exists between young and old, rich and poor and races of people, eliminating the separation issues between women and men can eliminate the polarity between everyone and everything.

When a man goes out with a woman for the first time, he generally tries to make the best impression that he can. He puts on his best clothing, takes her to the best restaurant and may even borrow his friend's car because it looks better than his car. He presents what he thinks is his best behavior, giving off a manly and confident appearance. He can be charming and polite, which are qualities that are attractive to women. He might even misrepresent the facts of his life to create a more favorable picture of himself.

What is the point in trying to establish a strong first impression that is false or not the real you? This is where things begin to go wrong. The history of romance has proven that men do not live up to that first impression. Why not be normal and natural? Why wouldn't you want women to accept you as you are? Women also help set themselves up to be let down because they look for men to impress them in the beginning of the relationship. It gets worse when men start making excuses for the illusion they have created when they can not live up to that first impression.

When people stay in relationships based on false pretenses, it usually leads to false expectations, misunderstanding and conflict. Making promises and painting false pictures about who you are, what you've done and what you intend to do without backing your statements up with action is part of what keeps women and men in disharmony. Most people don't want to deal with the reality inside a relationship. Instead of separating, deception now becomes a part of the union. How can a healthy, sound relationship develop, when its seeds are deception and conflict?

Deception generally leads to confrontation. A man should never physically challenge a woman. It shows a lack of understanding of the male role and is the result of improper guidance while growing up. Often a woman's only defense is her words. Usually a man who is physically abusive refuses to listen to a woman's opinion. This is the time when honest communication is necessary. If a couple can't discuss the issues calmly, a man should be mentally strong enough to allow the situation to cool off. Only after he has calmed down can he discuss things objectively.

Whenever there are issues between a man and a woman, and the man loses control, it's usually a reflection on the man, regardless of the circumstances.

Whenever a relationship is rocky and the couple stays together, it is also a reflection on the man. This reflection on men is the same as the universal law, for every action there's an equal and opposite reaction. In other words, women are reacting to what men do.

Difficulties exist to be learned from and overcome. When you lose control while dealing with a challenge, nothing gets resolved and sometimes the challenge turns into a problem that continues to grow. If you sense that you are not coming from a place of love, self-introspection is the next step. Why are you acting this way? What is it that you really want? If you can not address the situation honestly, you maintain your connection to the drama and the drama continues.

Whatever a woman does to disrupt a relationship reflects on the man's weaknesses. In general as men get weaker, women get stronger.

The stronger a woman becomes, the more challenging she can be to a man who lacks strength. A man's shortcomings make it difficult for him to address issues properly, or sever the relationship. This is an important reason why men must determine whether or not they are prepared to be with a potential mate for life. When this determination is made, it makes sense to slow down and pay attention to how things feel and act accordingly. This honest approach creates the best that can be gotten out of any relationship. Without honesty it's just a matter of time before the relationship fails.

It is very difficult for a woman to sever a relationship with a man she cares about. It takes a lot of unhappiness for the average woman to leave a man. Within the same context, if a man is being disruptive, he needs to be able to straighten himself out or find a partner suited to his character. The degree of character a man possesses has a positive effect on the mate he attracts and how successful things can turn out. Since women choose men, men balance a woman's choice by putting their best effort into making the relationship work.

Most women naturally think of their children and mate when they think of issues that affect their family. As husbands and fathers, men should also think of the welfare of the family first. This is what the word family means. Remember the *three musketeers*, one for all and all for one! Without this understanding, the family can not be a cohesive unit.

It is necessary for fathers to talk with and teach children, even if they are not involved with the mother. Mothers can not and should not have to raise the children in their care alone, especially boys! It is important for fathers to become more involved with the boys, especially when the rites of passage from boyhood into manhood arrives. This happens when boys turn 13 years of age. At this time a father must discuss with his mate the importance of letting the boys grow into manhood. A mother must untie the apron strings and allow the male influence of the father to become the dominant force in a boy's life.

Boys must be taught at an early age to respect females in and outside of the family. Life is a learning process and learning how to respect girls can
help to offset serious relationship challenges in later years.

Our society does not teach boys to be responsible. By the time many young men actually begin to think and act responsibly, they might be in their forties or fifties. Some never do. Therefore the gift of manhood does not get cultivated or passed on to the next generation.

One of the first lessons that fathers need to teach the boys in their care is the importance of ones intent. They need to be taught at an early age how to observe and predict the consequences of their intent. Their observations will allow them to realize that negative intentions will always produce negative results, and negative results produce pain. After feeling enough pain that follows negative intent, hopefully they will begin to appreciate the importance of thinking positive. When men learn to think with positive intent, women will respond in kind.

Many men are not honest about their intent and thus have taken away the gift that rightfully belongs to themselves and a partner – the gift of each other. It is the same as not being true to yourself. If you are not true to yourself, you alter yourself by creating a false image of who you naturally are. This disrupts your harmony with yourself and subsequently the harmony with a mate. Much too often we lose ourselves and in the process lose our significant other because we are not discussing our feelings or acting out the feelings that we claim.

Can you imagine a relationship with a woman whose spirit is free and flowing naturally? Can you imagine what kind of world we could live in if women were not struggling for the right to be considered equal with men? This is why the frustrations that women have continue, because too often men have not lived up to the challenge to be the best that they can be.

It is often said, "I'm not my brother's keeper." Of course you are your brother's keeper, as is every man old enough to understand that life is a learning experience and that we are all learning from each other. We are all connected, all a part of the same reality, the same truth, living in one world created by the one Creator. Women instinctively understand this truth. This is why they bring men the challenges from their previous relationships. It's the same as collectively telling men what they are doing keeps relationships off balance.

It is natural for you to be your sister's or brother's keeper, since whatever affects one affects all. If you are interested in developing a relationship with a woman, you have a responsibility to help her resolve the challenges of her past with patience. You first have the responsibility of resolving your own issues with patience. If you are not ready to resolve your own issues, how can you assist anyone else?

When a woman falls in love for the first time, her mindset is usually open and giving. When she discovers her Prince Charming is not such a prince, she usually becomes disappointed, closed and guarded.

When a man can help a woman address past disappointments, he is demonstrating one of the traits of a responsible teacher. We learn from pain everyday, yet it is the caring and grounded person that attempts to turn the pain into joy, and this individual deserves our admiration. This sets some people apart from those who are oblivious to the pitfalls of other people. When we continue to create pain while disregarding the creation of joy, we disrupt our lives and the lives of those around us.

When you demonstrate that you value a woman enough to help turn her pain into joy, you help her to build faith and trust in herself and in you. You will not only receive her love, but her gratitude as well.

In the corporate world, qualified experts are hired to research problems and come back with answers. Our elected officials need to send qualified experts into our communities to research what keeps women and men from achieving happiness and how to resolve the challenges faced when raising children.

You get an owner's manual every time you spend money for an electrical appliance. Relationships are far more important than appliances. Where are the manuals on relationships, how to treat ourselves, how to treat women, and how to raise children?

We can not control the lives of children, but if we properly educate and guide them during the early stages of their lives, we have helped them take steps in the right direction. We have then planted seeds that grow flowers, instead of the seeds that grow thorns.

The proper balance between being a parent and being a friend is essential, and it requires sincere dialogue between parents and children.

The relationship between a coach and an athlete might be the model to emulate, especially when considering the interaction between a father and son. The teaching should be relaxed and casual in order to be assimilated with love. This approach helps the student to see that the teacher cares which makes learning fun and can avoid resistance. Thinking as a coach (guide) helps parents to teach children through example. Parents will not be as inclined to apply pressure while teaching children. It will also help for parents to discuss this concept with children so that everyone is clear about the process.

If fathers are not around to teach sons, grandfathers can fill the role of father. Some grandfathers will be able to address issues that were not addressed when raising their own sons. In the absence of father and grandfather, uncles, cousins or close male friends should help with raising boys in a positive way.

Young boys have everything within them to become responsible men, yet achieving this end result is not automatic. Growing up does not make a male a man; this quality has to be cultivated. It is the degree to which we mature and meet challenges that qualifies and constitutes manhood. In contrast, young girls have latent attributes within them that allow them to grow into responsible women. Womanhood is automatic because of the womb that creates life within a woman's body. Love is also solidified within all women and love is the quality that maintains the universe. How else could women give birth to the planet? Women are capable of saving the planet because of the natural nurturing qualities inherent in their nature. However, our society has ignored the vibration of love and this oversight makes nurturing difficult.

Most men think that women are weaker than they are. This misconception helps men to believe that they can take advantage of women. Contrary to many peoples belief, all women are potentially strong. They are biologically superior to men. This is not as noticeable when we see frail, passive women taking mental and physical abuse from big brawny men. The tendency is to think and believe that these women are weak. But the mere fact that they can withstand that kind of abuse speaks clearly of their actual strength.

All men are not strong. Physical strength doesn't constitute real inner strength. Strength is exemplified when a man consciously addresses issues, big and small, which are put before him for resolution. Without higher consciousness we are weak and susceptible to destructive and addictive behavior.

When we are addicted, we lack will power and selfishness predominates. We look outside of ourselves and try to avoid dealing with what's happening inside of us. The end result of all this external and internal chaos is our wandering around in a circle of confusion like a dog following its tail.

Many of us pay professionals or attend clinics in an attempt to understand the challenges and control the addictions. Yet the answers are within us! It is just a matter of turning our attention inward so we don't bring pain to children, mates or ourselves.

The respect and appreciation that should be given to women can be seen in the question,

"What came first, the chicken or the egg?" This is an age-old question asked by scholars and laymen alike. I used to believe the chicken came first for two outstanding reasons. The Creator shows us that chickens have been given the privilege of laying eggs, and the sum can never be greater than the source. You cannot get fifty cents from a quarter and you will not find a child giving birth to a grown up. In the same way, a chicken was needed to lay the egg, not the egg laying the chicken. I remember feeling especially proud when a friend of mine told me that Socrates also believed that the chicken came first.

14

However, I have since evolved to understand that they both arrived at the same time. You could not have one without the other; they are different degrees of the same thing. For the same reason, I believe that female and male were once one being.

We pass through mothers in order to take the first breath. This explains why mothers are special. But why do we each believe that it's just our own mothers who are so special? Doesn't everybody have a mother? Isn't every woman a potential mother?

All women should be considered special. This understanding if applied automatically makes us all special.

Let's learn the lesson that we should be teaching boys in our care. If a man takes advantage of a woman, he is acting out a message that says it's alright for someone to do the same thing to the women he loves. This approach maintains the separation of the sexes by continuing the cycle of abuse.

Men who are in touch with all aspects of themselves including their feminine side are more likely to move forward in harmony with women.

Men who remain asleep and choose to cling to outdated beliefs about gender will require help in order to step into the light. Men must learn to use the feminine right side of their brain, which is the intuitive and insightful side, as well as the masculine left side, which is the analytical and practical side. Because men have been mostly using the left side of their brain, they learn to see themselves and their actions as separate from nature and life. This is the side that wants to control everything, the side that's destroying the world because it has no balance, the side that uses the intellect to work things out.

Around 1990 Jacques Cousteau claimed that the earth's seas and oceans were dying. If the oceans die, so will the plankton and phytoplankton, which are the cornerstones to the food chain and a major source of oxygen for our planet. Add this dilemma to the present destruction of the earth's ozone layer, and we can see that human survival is at a critical stage right this moment! According to research, there may not be an ozone layer left ten-to-twenty years from now. And human beings cannot survive without it. John Harris, herbalist and health advocate, once said, "We are a society of cause without giving any concern to effect."

John Harris had a very popular health talk radio show on WBAI that came on an hour before the Gary Null show. In 1999, I talked to John about interviewing conscious minded people on his show. I suggested that he tell his listeners that they would be able to meet him and his quest the following day at a rented space. This would allow the guest speaker to share knowledge and sell alternative health products and services.

John liked the idea and suggested that I line up a few interviews to try things out. I contacted Dr. Delbert Blair to be John's first quest. I had known Dr. Blair for about three years and knew that he always left his audience satisfied and wanting more. He was very happy to be interviewed and made arrangements to fly to New York from Chicago. I than contacted Bob Frissell, "Nothing in This Book Is True But It's Exactly How Things Are" Leonard Orr "Breaking the Death Habit" and Professor Charles Finch, a noted historian and told them about the plan to share knowledge and alternative products. They were receptive and willing to be interviewed. Dr. Blair was a hit on the radio show and the following day he packed the 100 seat room. John and I were very excited about the collaboration and began to make plans to interview other quest. Unfortunately two weeks later, John unexpectantly passed away.

Pressing a button can now destroy all life. The more technologically advanced we become, the further away we move from the Creator. We have almost moved to the furthest point of our convoluted drama.

Everything is mental, everything is consciousness. The planet is sick and dying to the same extent that man is sick and dying. Our environment follows our consciousness. When man makes himself healthy mentally, physically and spiritually, the planet automatically follows suit. We will only succeed in doing this when the two halves become whole.

Women

A lot has been said, written and discussed concerning women and what makes them who they are. It is a common belief of men that women are mysterious, complex and hard to understand. Men also say that women can be very difficult about what men feel should be easy to deal with. It seems that the difficulty men experience results from the issues that women face when men challenge them.

A friend turned to me as we rode the elevator in my building and said, "Women have a lot of baggage." I looked at him and replied, "Men give them a lot of those bags."

The spontaneity in our remarks made us both laugh. When he finally caught his breath, he said, "Yeah, you're right." "And those bags are heavy, too," I said, which made us laugh again.

Whenever a woman's happiness is denied or hindered in any way, she reacts in ways that make men feel justified in calling her mysterious or too complicated to be understood. In other words, it seems men have trouble understanding women's unhappiness.

Most men are not aware that they initiate actions that are the root cause of whatever is happening in a relationship. Since men are the cause, they also have the cure. Since action and reaction are one and the same, men and women collectively do their part to create harmony or disharmony.

The way that women react to the actions of men and situations in general can determine whether they achieve happiness or unhappiness in a relationship. Despite the fact that men shape the world, women are held accountable for their actions, and they suffer when their reaction is not appropriate.

Women reacting to the actions of men do not mean that women don't think for themselves. Nor does it mean that women are not equal to men intellectually or are not responsible for their own actions. Everything has its opposite: act-react, love-hate, up-down. These opposites (duality) are all connected in the same

20

manner that females and males are essentially one and the same, just different degrees of the same thing. When this connection is understood, a condition can ensue capable of producing balance and peace of mind.

Many people believe that women initiate their own painful or pleasurable situations. If women were initiating action, it would mean they initiated their own inequality. It would also mean that men are reacting. If men are reacting to women, that would also mean women were and are the cause of all the drama that humanity faces. However the drill goes into the ground, not the ground into the drill.

The earth's axis tilts 23 ½ degrees. This tilt creates a wobble as the earth goes around the sun. It takes the earth 26,000 years to make one complete wobble. As the earth spins away from the center of the galaxy, people mentally fall asleep. As the earth turns the corner and moves back toward the center of the galaxy people begin to wake back up.

For the past 13,000 years this planet has been asleep, and the vibration of the planet was electric. We were in darkness and the quality of life was masculine. Electricity is masculine. Now the planet has awakened and moved into the light. The vibration of the planet is now magnetic. Magnetism is feminine. The progress that women are making is a direct result of the magnetic vibration of the planet and our transition from darkness into light.

Women are now entering into a unique period in time that calls for them to approach challenges in a different way. For example, using intelligence and intuition instead of emotions to respond to their condition. This approach creates productive results. Natural talents and abilities are more easily expressed. If women realize that they are special and accept it, they might find it easier to choose a man based on what they have discovered about themselves instead of what they might want for the wrong reasons.

Many women have made a conscious decision to be as aggressive as men, regardless of what they are trying to achieve. Thus, it appears that women are initiating situations while still reacting to what men are or are not doing. In addition to altering their feminine attributes, this aggressive response helps to push women and men further apart. It's the same as fighting a fire with more fire.

Many women also tend to depend too much on men to provide them with the happiness they believe they are entitled to. Yet, they often deny their dependency because they know that the system raised them to be dependent. As a result, women blame men for their unhappiness without considering the role that they play in their own journey. Women choose the men in their lives and the men they choose are reflections of themselves. When this truth is accepted, women will realize that giving love unconditionally is the answer that leads to their happiness. Why? Because whatever our consciousness accepts becomes our realty.

The birth cycle allows women to be instinctively drawn to priorities that have lasting value: happiness, children, love, peace, laughter, creativity, fun and so on. The lives growing within their bodies motivate women to think about and want those values in life that matter most. Women naturally vibrate at a higher consciousness; thus, they pay a higher price in pain and suffering when their thoughts are not positive. This is why the appropriate reaction and response to a man's action becomes extremely important to a woman's well being. Without the appropriate response, we fall into a pattern that keeps us repeating the same painful experience until we learn.

The priorities that women focus on can balance out the destructive pursuits of men. However, if women don't carefully choose the men they want to be with, they can easily become a part of the drama that men are drawn to. Women's natural priorities and values help men to get in touch with the side of themselves that acts responsibly. Men will not be able to do this without women's help. If a woman can calmly step back and allow a responsible man to observe himself without escalating the situation, she helps create the balance necessary for things to work themselves out.

In the not-too-distant past women were still not considered equal. Many women believed and accepted their second-class status. The women's suffrage movement of the late 1800's asserted some equality for women in terms of the law; however, most men refused to accept women as equals, and their condition remained basically the same.

As some of the wealthier families began sending their daughters to school for a higher education, things slowly began to change for the better, especially after women were granted the right to vote. It wasn't until the Civil Rights Movement in the 1960's, that the women's movement made real progress in terms of education and career opportunities.

This accelerated progress has placed women alongside men in the very competitive arena of the corporate world. This has been both positive and negative. Positive, because women have since taken giant strides in raising their economic status. Negative, because the corporate world can be a cold, dog-eat-dog battleground that breeds antihuman attitudes. In order for women to earn and maintain their positions of authority, they found themselves conforming to male values in the business world.

We can now see women competing and backstabbing each other in the same cold manner as men have done for centuries. Some female executives are ordering employees around without considering their feelings, creating undue pressure for the sake of quotas and demanding overtime from employees without regard for their families and other responsibilities. It is also unfortunate that the backstabbing and competing among women goes on outside the work place as well.

This type of situation affects everyone, especially children, because parents *are* not able to spend quality time with them. When the parents *are* around, they are usually stressed, too tired or too irritable because of the drama that takes place at work.

Slowly and surely, women have begun to lose those feminine attributes needed to maintain who they naturally are. The ideal situation is for women to be able to progress, while maintaining the integrity of their feminine qualities. Women will not be able to find happiness if they choose to act like men in order to compete with men.

In 1972 when I was in college, I copyrighted a series of poster concepts because I thought I saw where things were headed. I had ten drawings of women doing diverse things that men normally did. One of the posters had women in soldiers' uniforms, shooting guns in combat; another had a woman carrying a man over the threshold after the wedding; and another had women on a football field in uniform, warming up before the game. The words under each poster read, "You don't have to act like a man to get equal rights." I was trying to illustrate the futility of women striving for equality by acting like those who were preventing them from achieving their goals.

Despite popular opinion, the universe has complimentary and opposing attributes for both feminine and masculine principals. When a woman conceives, she carries her baby nine months for a reason. When the baby is born, the mother is there to nurse the baby for a reason. If women stop having babies because of their careers, life stands still. If every woman with children had a career, then fathers, family members, friends, agencies and strangers would have to become babysitters. It has become obvious that people cannot be trusted with the care of your family. Do women really want to go to work while the men stay home (house dad) with the children? Do women really want to take care of men financially and pay the bills too? Or, is their position simply a reaction to the way men have historically mistreated women?

I am not suggesting that women not have careers. I believe that women would not be fighting for the right to have careers if men were more responsible and women were less angry about things they don't approve of. If our economic and social systems did more regarding the importance of raising healthy families, it would complete the triangle that creates success in the household.

In order for women and men to meet the challenges they face successfully, they must work together and learn to appreciate the connection there is in all of creation. When we can, appreciating the connection between all things helps people work together to succeed. When we can accept the fact that there is nothing to hold on to, protect or control, it will help us let go of our insecurities and fears. When women can do this, they will instinctively not accept negative traits in men that lead to their unhappiness.

Every man that a woman meets represents some part of her masculine qualities that make up part of who she is. This aspect of her own duality, if understood, helps her to become balanced. When she encounters people that don't appeal to her, she can learn to view them as teachers, allowing her to see different sides of herself that she doesn't approve of. This approach allows women and men to respond differently to negative action. As we continue to respond negatively, pain will pursue us until we learn that it is ourselves that we see in the other person so that we accept and appreciate who we are.

Often people feel confused because of the pain in their life, especially when they feel they are positive thinkers with good intentions. It is our karma that is manifesting itself. The pain felt could be the result of pain perpetrated on someone else earlier or in another life. Free will allows us to practice Spiritual Law in order to learn and choose to experience joy instead of pain.

In December of 1999, I went to Trinidad and spent 20 days there. For someone who had spent most of his life in the concrete jungle of New York City, the mountainous greenery of Trinidad was a perfect relief. As I observed the system of the country, what really caught my attention was how much more aware and knowledgeable the women were than the men. The women talked about pursuing education, jobs, plans to get ahead and what they were doing to achieve their goals. The men talked about sports, having fun, getting high and what they were going to do to get ahead.

When I returned to America, I realized that the same conditions exist here as in Trinidad. It was not as noticeable because of the overcrowded environment of the large cities and the rapid pace of everything. These conditions do not allow one to stand back and easily observe what is going on. I began to believe that women are probably more aware and knowledgeable in most other countries.

It is common knowledge that girls are more mature and advanced mentally than boys are. It's a fact that women's brains fully develop earlier than men's do. However, with time and in harmony with themselves, men reach the same level of maturity as women. The present conditions of society imply that men still have a lot of catching up to do. Men will catch up with women when they work on developing the nurturing side of themselves. The Chinese illustrate this point with their concept of yin and yang (female/male balance).

In spite of the progress that women have made in the last hundred years, the inequality that exists between the sexes is still deeply rooted. Boys are raised to believe that they are lucky to have been born boys instead of girls. Later on in life, this way of thinking psychologically plays a part in their mistreatment of women.

To turn things around women might collectively turn their attention away from their negative reactions to men. This will yield the best results for everyone. Some women may find this hard to believe, but most men are not really aware of the harm that they cause. They actually think that what they do is expected of them in the name of a distorted sense of manhood. If they could see their reflections, they would be surprised to see how their actions affect the women in their lives.

Deep down inside most women know that the majority of men have a lot to learn and are not really aware of the harm they cause. Unfortunately the frustration that women feel because of what men do has created so much anger in women that they have made throwing wood on an already burning fire an art. Many women also have not been taught how to choose a man and make their choices without knowing whether or not a man has the ability to maintain a stable relationship.

Although it is perceived by many that there is equality between the sexes, the system was designed to favor males and continues to do so. Many things are still grossly unequal, while an illusion of equality remains. Many young women and men are confused by this deception. Young people have an inner sense that things are not right so they rebel without purpose or direction. After a brief moment of rebellion, they eventually conform to the status quo, never finding the answers they need.

Despite the fact that most sectors of society are designed to support the division between the sexes, women and men need to help each other bridge this artificial divide. This is the only way balance can be achieved, and balance equals harmony which results in happiness.

A woman's reaction to whatever men do or don't do can make a big difference in how things turn out. No woman can help the relationship work if she blindly accepts mistreatment from a man just because they are in a relationship. Women must peacefully challenge men to deal with whatever the issues are. This approach helps men to avoid using abuse as a method to resolve the differences.

If women are in the light, they can help show men the light. If a man is not receptive, she should consider moving on. Many young women try to alter the character of the men they want to be with. Most of us know this never works. Before she can lift him up, he'll pull her down. Why stick around for personal reasons and play a game that bears serious emotional consequences? A man left alone to reflect on the shortcomings will have a better chance of working things out.

It was mentioned to me that a wise old woman once said, "If a man treats you with love and respect, he's worth the time. If he mistreats you or doesn't respect you, move on because you deserve better. If you don't move on, you will deserve what you get. After three chances to work things out, a woman must seriously begin to work on a plan to save herself."

When a woman severs a relationship, it sends a serious message to the man that could not have been delivered had she stayed. If he understands what the issues are, he can provide some answers. If he doesn't understand, she did herself a favor and saved herself a lot of pain.

When men act inappropriately and women overlook it and make excuses for them, they think this is the most loving thing they can do for "the man." In reality it is the most destructive thing they can do to themselves, men and society.

Women reflect men, and when men act badly, it is made increasingly worse when women support and condone this behavior. If women collectively understood how to use their power, they would not put up with men who act inappropriately just because a romantic relationship has been established. They would move on to greener pastures without bitterness and would naturally attract men worthy of them. Men would than be forced to see the shortcomings and own up to the responsibilities.

Women accepting this kind of responsibility would automatically improve the lives of children, as everything the parents do is reflected in the child. Ending this cycle of abuse is one of the most important and loving things women can do for themselves and family.

It is important for women to stay positive and not succumb to fear, guilt or selfishness, the byproducts of low self-esteem. These are negative illusions, and if women refuse to accept them as part of the reality they will yield positive results in life. When this is done, women will have maintained a position that helps men to measure up to the best within themselves.

Many times it appears that women overreact to men's mistakes and mistreatment. It seems that when a man mistreats a woman, she reciprocates it back to him five times. It's as if she's remembering the other four men who had previously mistreated her. A woman lives in the past with this approach. She is laying a foundation for her own future pain and suffering. She has created negative karma for herself and deposited it into her bank of life which she must account for. The debt must be paid. She is about to be mistreated five times for that debt and for as many more times that she did not forgive the previous offenders.

For a moment, imagine all the negative deposits a woman who thinks this way has in the bank account. Can she sincerely state that she wants peace of mind and happiness? If she does, she must forgive the offender with or without his accompanying apology.

Forgiveness is the most powerful and loving thing one can give because everything in the outside world is just a reflection of you. It is yourself you have forgiven and if you cannot forgive yourself, you cannot love yourself. If you cannot love yourself, you cannot expect anyone else to love you. When you can sincerely forgive, you vibrate on a higher frequency and affect everyone with your vibration.

If addicts would hustle business in the same way they hustle to feed the addictions, they would all be wealthy. Similarly, if women would put the same energy into themselves (unselfishly) that they put into trying to establish equality with men, equality would be realized.

Women who compete with men and try to measure up to the standards that men have set for themselves will never establish equality. "Sex kittens" who cater to men will also not be able to establish equality with this approach. Women must go inside themselves for answers and not allow anyone else's point of view to become their reality.

Nurturing a good relationship is an important initial step towards establishing equality with a man.

Women should discuss with girls in their care what to look for when choosing a boyfriend. A girl's first serious experience with romance usually occurs with a boy who attends the same school. Girls are attracted to boys who are cute, popular, dress well, dance well, excel at sports, drive a car, have money, and for a host of other superficial reasons. These are not the qualities that make good relationships. These are the qualities that help create big alter egos. Boys who are interested in getting to know who you are and how you think have a better chance at creating a good relationship. A cute face, a fancy car or a nice wardrobe is not the blueprint for happiness.

While on her journey, a young woman can learn to hold men responsible for what they say and do. If what is said is not backed up by what is done, something is wrong. Women must hold men accountable for what they do and what they say. If women are not willing to do this, they set themselves up to be hurt by men who don't have women's best interest at heart.

Have you noticed the similarities between little girls and elderly women? Both can be very sweet, giving and concerned about the welfare of others. However, between the ages of sixteen and sixty, women tend to be more concerned with their own welfare. The selfishness, possessiveness and lack of responsibility that men exemplify have caused women to act the same way. They are overly concerned about being abused, and begin to become selfish and guarded.

As mothers talk with daughters about how to avoid some of the pain that they previously experienced, mothers must also address the issues that create a state of present-day emotional pain for themselves.

Quite often couples find themselves arguing about the simplest things. Couples who argue a lot are usually trying to prove that one person's point of view is right and the other person's point of view is wrong. Two days later, they can not recall why they argued. It doesn't matter who was right or who was wrong. The issue is that they argue at all. It doesn't matter what they argue about.

My grandfather used to say to my grandmother that either she's too smart for him or he's not strong enough for her. The fact that a man argues with a woman about a point of view implies that he lacks confidence in himself. Even if his point of view is correct, he takes credibility away from himself when he feels he has to argue about it.

It is apparent at birth that female and male are complete opposites. The reproductive organs of a woman are inside the body, while the reproductive organs of a man are outside the body. This distinctive difference is consistent with everything associated with females and males. Women are internal and men are external. This represents how it is, mentally, emotionally and physically.

Women have the ability and potential to succeed at the highest levels. Unfortunately, not enough men are supporting them. Many men are full of insecurities, low self-esteem and petty jealousies. These types of men have a history of holding women back and destroying the potential to accomplish goals through control methods.

Most women cannot succeed with a mate like this. The few who do are truly exceptional. The others who do not succeed might have achieved success had they found support from a significant other. Men should learn to support a mate, given that whatever one does for the other, one also does for self.

Have you ever really noticed the difference between little girls and little boys? Little girls even at one and two years of age, are already little women, it's automatic! All they need to do is grow up past puberty; it's their birthright. In contrast, little boys at that same age are still immature. Teenage boys, even at eighteen and nineteen, exhibit childish behavior. Grown men can be as old as sixty and behave immaturely. Manhood is a cultivated quality. It is not automatic!

Many men believe that the choice of a mate is theirs, yet women are the ones who do the actual choosing. It's just like being at a party and walking across the room to ask a woman for a dance. While he is doing the asking, she is the one who makes the choice. If she says yes, he gets to dance with her. If she says no, he is left to walk back across the room.

While the privilege of choosing is a woman's, a man has the opportunity to see to it that the relationship works. Therein lies the balance. I believe women instinctively understand that men determine whether a relationship succeeds or fails. This could be why most women are more concerned with how men feel about them than how they feel about a particular man. Once a relationship is consummated, it creates a bond between the couple that tends to be stronger in the female; she is more nurturing and concerned about building a stable family unit. If relationships between women and men fall apart, women always pay a higher price as they have more to lose. When there are children involved, they are usually left with the mother who in a sense must now become mother and father. A woman has to find a job if she isn't working, or has to leave a job if she is working. To make matters worse, we live in a world where a woman's physical look determines how much attention and interest she is likely to receive from others. Yet, the ability to think and reason have nothing to do with how someone looks.

Many of us are concerned with the amount of time we have instead of what we do with that time. Most of us think we waste time because we have not been taught how to utilize it. Yet there is no such thing as wasting time. It looks like we are wasting time because we keep going around in circles doing the same thing over and over again. We lock ourselves into a pattern of thinking and unless we change the pattern things remain the same. We begin to believe there is not enough time in a day to do what we would like to do. The Creator makes no mistakes. Twenty-four hours in a day is perfect.

A woman I know was going out with a man for about three months when she announced that she had become pregnant. The following week, she did not want to see him again. It seems that this man had been telling a few women that they were his one and only. One of the women found the phone numbers for the others and called them all to find out what was going on. These phone calls revealed the extent to which this man was incapable of being honest and responsible with any of them. These women had not given themselves the opportunity to really get to know him and possibly learn what type of man he was before getting involved. In spite of what was revealed about his dishonesty, some of these women continued to date him. Some women tend to stay in relationships like this, hoping that they will be the ones to change a man. In the long run, many women find out that they have given a man ammunition that becomes a weapon to use against them when they stay.

When you buy a car, you take the time to look under the hood to make sure the car has an engine, a transmission, a tight set of brakes and other essentials. You might bring a mechanic to thoroughly examine the car before you pay for it. If women were to adopt this attitude when seeking a partner, there would be a lot less unhappy and frustrated women. Many women spend more time trying to pick out the right dress or the right pair of shoes than they do trying to pick out the right man. It's more difficult to choose a man than a car or a pair of shoes because you need to know if he has the mindset you desire before you commit yourself.

Rushing into relationships is like going to Las Vegas to try and win money; the odds are stacked against you. You must also allow a man to learn about you and what you want in a relationship. Getting caught up in a deceptive game of keeping things about yourself from someone until you feel you have that person hooked is like digging a hole from which you can not easily escape. Finding a responsible, caring and loving person is the exception, not the rule. Give yourself the best chance to succeed by being open about yourself and asking your potential mate to do the same.

Children

The greatest creative achievement on earth is giving birth to another living being. The memories that a mother has of the child are just as important as the child's memories of the mother. Life is memory and memory is composed of our experiences.

When a father is present at the birth of the child, he becomes as much a part of the creative process as the mother and child. This collective experience helps to strengthen the family bond. Husbands and fathers would be more inclined to successfully meet the challenges that disrupt family life if they saw the fruit of their seed delivered into the world.

During childbirth, mothers are told to lie on their backs in order to give birth. This position goes against gravity and makes childbirth very painful. As a result of this and other reasons, cesarean births are performed on women and accepted as a normal way to give birth.

The pain and difficulty associated with giving birth to a child, coupled with the emotional and physical scars left after a cesarean birth creates unfavorable feelings in many women wanting to become pregnant. Birth is the first major experience a mother and child will have with each other. Only the mother knows her thoughts when she looks at the children and remembers the pain associated with their births. What are her thoughts when she looks at the scars across her abdomen that resulted from her efforts to bring a child into the world?

For thousands of years, indigenous women all over the world instinctively knew that the way to give birth was to stand on their feet and squat down to deliver. This position allows gravity to assist in bringing forth the child. Today, natural and holistic communities are advocating squatting down in pools of water (distilled) in order to give birth naturally.

For nine months, the developing child feeds and breathes through the mother's umbilical cord. When the baby is born, it should remain attached to its mother's umbilical cord for at least two to three hours. This is done to allow the baby to adjust to breathing on its own. It's a shock to a baby's entire system when the umbilical cord is cut prematurely. It's a further shock to a baby's system when she or he is smacked on the behind at birth to induce breathing.

In truth, proper breathing is the key to a healthy and balanced life. Human beings have not yet learned how to breathe correctly. Within the holistic community, there are classes in yoga, reiki and rebirthing to help us learn how to breathe correctly.

Children are gifts that come through us; we do not own them and they do not belong to us. We have a responsibility to guide them accurately in all matters of growth and development. This cannot be done if we approach children as if they are property. This approach does not allow for freedom of thought. If parents assert control over children instead of guiding them, their minds will not develop to their fullest creative potential. You personalize the relationship when you think you own them. When you personalize anything, you evaluate it based on what it means to you as opposed to what it means to itself.

47

A friend of mine once said that her child is a part of her, which makes the relationship intrinsically personal. This is true to some extent. However, consciously personalizing the relationship with the child is the problem. She asked, "To whom does the child belong if not the parents?" The child belongs to the Universe and to itself. Some parents might interpret this to mean that they are not to be held accountable for loving and raising children. This is not the case at all. We must still be responsible and loving parents. We must also allow the child to understand this method of child rearing at an early age. Parents should not underestimate children by thinking they are too young to learn and understand.

If we personalize the relationship with children, we justify indulging or abusing them. Spoiling or beating children does not prepare them to be positive - thinking adults. The pain and unhappiness that people experience in childhood follow them into adult life. When children are given everything they want from parents, they will expect the same from other people. Other people are not going to cater to children or grown adults as parents do. The temper tantrums that children indulge in create pain and unhappiness when those same tantrums occur in adults.

Many parents who spoil children are not aware of the damage they do. Parents often cater to every situation instead of relaxing and trusting a child's instincts to know and define his or her own interests. Much too often you hear, "Do you want this?... Do you want that?... Are you sure?"

It is better to allow children to make their own decisions (with your guidance) and take the initiative to reach out to you and show you what they like or want to do. Nature is in their corner and on their side! Intuitively they know when it's time for their next lesson in life. They are destined to experience the journey that they have to take. When you allow children to practice decision making, when they become adults they will likely make wise choices. Your responsibility lies in showing them the right road. You cannot walk the road for them, or control their destiny regardless of your love, devotion, or fear.

There are parents who sincerely believe that they have a right to spoil children. They usually believe that catering to children is a harmless endeavor. We

49

have all seen examples of parents who allow children to boss them around instead of instructing children and pointing them in the right direction, especially single parents who are raising children by themselves. In some cases, single mothers indulge children in an attempt to compensate for the father's absence. Without a father figure around, a spoiled child can make a mother's life miserable.

Women raising children alone cannot continue to be the foundation in which children grow into adults, especially male children. An indulged boy who grows into a man tends to look for a woman who will continue to spoil him. This makes it difficult for him to create happiness with a woman.

Any potential mate a single mother chooses must give the same love and attention to the children that he gives to her. A single mother must take the time to find out whom she is letting into the family's life. Quite often the media reports horror stories about single parents who did not take the time to learn about someone they wanted to share their lives with. Women who accepted men who did not care about them or the children usually told these horror stories.

Many women walk away from relationships because they claim the man is looking for a mother, not a wife. Most men who murder wives or girlfriends are men whose mothers refused to cut the figurative umbilical cord. In most cases these women were murdered because they either tried to leave a dysfunctional relationship or they were caught having an affair. A vicious cycle is repeated from generation to generation when women are left alone to raise sons, who will one day leave women who will have to again raise sons alone because of man's failure to be responsible.

Single mothers should have a statue erected to them for having raised children alone. However, they must maintain discipline when it comes to their sons. When they tell sons, "No," they can not let them talk them into saying, "Yes," two minutes later. This will mix up the roles and have the mother acting like the child and the child acting like the parent. This can lead to a confused and insecure child or a dominating and demanding one.

I have heard mothers and fathers refer to daughters as mommy, ma, mom and sons as pops, dad, popi. These signals are misleading and could lead to confusion if continued. Children are still children and should be encouraged to be comfortable in this once-in-a-lifetime experience.

There are times when a mother and father tell the young son that he is the man of the house, while he is still enjoying how to be a boy. Why rush sons into manhood without the lessons that allow them to become responsible men? If the statement is made to feed his little ego, he receives a false sense of who he really is. If he did try to act like the man of the house, it would turn into a joke at his expense.

You are the children's guide. If you accept and maintain the role as a guide, you will learn just as much from them as they learn from you. The children will love you just as much if you prepare them to realize their potential without spoiling them.

If a parent is not confident in the role of guide, the parent can visit friends and relatives who are raising well-balanced children and question them about their methods. Parents can also inquire about recommended books and classes on proper parenting. It is the responsibility of a parent to learn how to be the best parent possible. If you raise well-balanced children, you help to create well-balanced grandchildren. Everything you do with your children extends for generations.

Some parents believe that beating a child is a necessary part of raising a child. There are parents who know that it is wrong to physically abuse children but they can't seem to control themselves. In many cases the beatings are the result of a lack of knowledge, patience and understanding by the parent. It's like abusing the child for the knowledge you lack about raising a child.

When you physically discipline children, you are likely preparing them to mistreat the future children in their care. Many of these beatings and the acceptance of them are associated with love. We believe our parents loved us, so it must be all right for us to beat or abuse those we love. There are relationships where women physically abuse men, and the men accept this because their mothers loved and beat them.

Spoiling or beating children are two extremes that are not in their best interest. There are parents that actually do both. One minute they are indulging the child, and the next minute they are abusing the child.

Can you imagine the confusion going on in a child's mind; not knowing how to respond to situations, insecure about little things, and mixed up about most things?

Many parents try to relive their lives vicariously through children because they are dissatisfied with the outcome of their own lives. This mindset helps to create the situation that has parents spoiling or abusing them. Everything the spoiled child does is great. Compliments flow even when unjustified. Everything the abused child does is never good enough. All attempts at progress and self-improvement are criticized.

In both extremes, children receive a false impression of who they are and what they are capable of. The indulged child accepts the impression of being great and feeds off this false impression of reality. The abused child develops low self-esteem or fights back and remains hostile.

Quite often, the self-esteem of abused children is low because they are made to feel guilty when they do not perform well enough. They are often told that they will never amount to much, or they are beaten and abused for rebelling against the domination of the parents.

When parents harass children, many children consciously and unconsciously fail at what they try to accomplish. Many of these failures lead to problems in later life because parents unknowingly drive children into a life of emotional pain. This pain usually finds a form of release when people strike back at society.

It is obvious that such parents did not quite understand how to best raise children, but for adults to continue to blame parents for their failures does not help them resolve their issues.

When parents responsible for your care were raising you, they were responsible for your guidance and well being. Now that you are an adult, parental responsibility cease and parents now become mother and father, two people who gave birth to you.

As an adult, when you consider a mother and father as parents, it implies that they are still responsible for you. You are now responsible for yourself and the children you raise until they are grown. The control the abusive parents had or still have, over your life, can be broken if you understand that they are not your caretakers anymore. Love and forgive them for your sake. They most likely had a strict upbringing, especially if they grew up in an old fashioned moralistic era. Blaming them, holding grudges or feeling sorry for yourself does not help you.

You should prepare yourself to raise children with love. You can not expect to raise healthy balanced children if your brain is full of negative memories about the parents who raised you. Remind yourself daily that every day is a new beginning. Realize that parents that raised you did it based on what they knew. Perhaps they had rough lives and did not know better.

There are parents who spoil daughters in the same way they spoil sons. Indulging girls is not as harmful as indulging boys because by nature women tend to be less destructive than men. This does not mean that parents should think that it is okay to spoil daughters. Women who are not spoiled will have a greater sense of independence and a better chance to raise a stable family. However, when women are catered to and act destructively, they have more behavioral issues than men.

Women who were indulged as children will most likely want to be catered to as adults. Some men don't mind spoiling the women they love. However, problems arise when a man begins a relationship spoiling a mate and for whatever reason, stops. A man who is not in love will not be willing to continue to indulge a mate. When the spoiling stops, it is not easy for a woman to accept the change. She begins to feel neglected, unloved, and sometimes becomes suspicious of a mate which creates more challenges. Eventually it's just a matter of time before the relationship breaks down.

There are many parents who mean well and sacrifice themselves in order to achieve the best for children. Parents should not believe that their life is over because they are raising children. Your life is just as precious as the child's life. The lives of you and the children are supposed to complement each other. You should maintain a proper balance between your needs and theirs.

I have a friend who happens to be a brilliant person and potentially, a great businessman. His understanding of spiritual knowledge is also very impressive. My friend is the father of a son. When the son was 5 years of age, the father began to put large sums of his earnings aside for the son's future. Over the years I mentioned the significance of investing the money in himself as a way of securing the son's future. I would especially bring up the conversation whenever I was aware that he was going through difficult times financially. He never agreed, so I ceased to mention the subject.

Instead of the son learning business from the father and from the father's ability to make confident, decisive decisions, the son was learning through osmosis how to be apprehensive and avoid taking risks. Even if the father failed in the business endeavors, he still would have been leaving the son far more than he started out with. The son would then be motivated to create his own financial path, not to mention the priceless intangibles the son would learn from the father's ability to take risks.

When we teach children by example, they learn quickly and are able to develop whatever they learn to a level that we can only dream about. There are many examples of people at the highest levels who were educated by observing the parent's involvement in business at an early age. The earlier children are exposed to the parents' expertise, the greater their potential to excel will be.

Have you noticed how intelligent babies are at birth? Their little minds are able to grasp and absorb things with incredible speed. Every mother I have heard talk about a baby believes that her super intelligent child is one of a kind. All mothers are correct about their child's brilliance. Children continue to learn and develop this mental gift until they reach seven or eight years of age. At this point, the ability to understand and learn seems to get slowed down. In some cases, it seems as if it has stopped altogether. The school system is largely responsible for this stagnation. The schools are not teaching children at the level of their ability to learn, and this stifles their creative imaginations.

When you consider all of the issues associated with finding the right mate, putting girls and boys in the same school at an early age is another basis for creating bad relationships. Boys are not as mature as girls and it takes time for boys to catch up. Teenage boys are not ready mentally or emotionally to deal with teenage girls who are more mature and in search of love.

Teenage pregnancy is a serious problem. Few teenagers of either sex can deal with a pregnancy without depending on the parents. Unfortunately, most boys and many girls don't provide parental care for the children at all. This creates a situation where parents of the girls find that they are acting as the parents of the grandchildren as well. Many times the mother of the child comes into conflict with her own mother on how the child should be raised. During these trying times, many fathers want to go back to hanging out with the fellas instead of being a responsible parent.

Our school system has not effectively educated or prepared students to deal with pregnancy or how to handle many of life's challenges. Instinctively, students realize that the school system is not teaching them what they need to know in order to succeed in life. This is why there are so many bored and delinquent students in schools. Academic comparisons of students in industrialized countries also show that American students are on the bottom half of the list.

If students cannot have their minds fed with the information that their intelligence demands, their minds will eventually acquire the *wrong* information. That is why many schools resemble police stations with armed guards and metal detectors to keep students from harming each other and teachers. In spite of these precautions, violence among students has gotten worse. Unless parents and concerned adults get involved, armed guards will continue to be necessary.

Parents should take an active role in order to learn more about children's interests and provide books focusing on those areas. Children tend to be indecisive and change their minds about what they originally wanted to learn. Parents should provide different kinds of information and cater to them in those new areas of interest. Parents should also expose children to real life experiences in the environment the children show an interest in.

Parents should join forces to challenge the school system about the content of children's education. More and more families are teaching children at home and achieving excellent results. These children tend to excel both in school and in life as they are taught to think freely and creatively. Our school system does not teach students how to think. Our system trains students how to conform.

Raising children is supposed to be a blessing. Yet, there are far too many parents giving children up for adoption, too many mothers having abortions and too many children becoming wards of the state. Street drugs, pharmaceutical drugs and chemicals put in the food we eat have helped to create a mindset that is not taking the welfare of children into consideration.

According to the Citizens Commission on Human Rights, the U.S. National Institute of Mental Health stated that 17 million school children around the world are taking psychiatric drugs.[1] Of the 17 million, 10 million are in the United States. The harsh reality is that, due to these drugs, precious young lives all over the country are at serious risk of being either permanently damaged or lost.

The Commission further stated that 80 billion dollars was budgeted for mental health care and more than six billion dollars was spent on mental health

---

[1] Citizens Commission on Human Rights: Fight For Kids, fightforkids.org/facts.html

research. Yet, we are witnessing unprecedented violent crimes among children, one of the world's worst scholastic records, an increase in drug abuse and teen suicides tripling since the 1960's.

The Commission also reports that these drugs are not medicines, but powerful mind-altering drugs, which can have very serious side effects and withdrawal symptoms. In its diagnostic manual, the American Psychiatric Association admits that a major complication of withdrawal from Ritalin (the most commonly prescribed psychiatric drug for children) is suicide. If they know and understand this fact, why is Ritalin still being given to America's youth?

Today's children need proper guidance more than children in the past did. When yesterday's children got into mischief, it was children's mischief. When today's children get into trouble, it is on an adult level: robbery, murder, rape and other crimes that are commonly associated with grown - ups.

In Florida a 13 year-old boy was accused of shooting a 35 year-old teacher in the head. The teacher died. The news broadcast stated that prosecutors were trying to determine if they should try the minor on the charge of murder as an adult.

In New York on the same news broadcast, a 16 year-old boy had been charged with cutting an 18 year-old multiple times with a box cutter. The 16 year-old, along with the mother and another adult, were charged with assault. According to the news, the mother and an adult male friend had prodded the fight, encouraging the young man to use the box cutter as they watched the fight with a bunch of neighborhood youths.

The next day, the Ted Koppel show focused on the 13 year-old boy who had been charged with murdering a teacher in front of other students. Ted Koppel interviewed two men on whether the boy should be tried and treated as an adult or as a minor. The two men advocated opposing positions regarding how much time the boy should receive for the crime. They both eventually agreed that possibly the law should be changed in the State of Florida to allow the courts to give to minors the same sentences they give to adults.

These problems with children have gotten so out of control that elected officials are trying to enact laws to allow children to be prosecuted as adults. How can we justify prosecuting children as adults? It's the same as placing blame on children for the world that we have created for them to live in.

Is it possible that we might be programming children to accept violence with the nursery rhymes we teach them? *Humpty Dumpty, Jack & Jill, Three Blind Mice and Rockabye Baby* are a few examples of nursery rhymes with violent themes. Let us take into consideration the violent video games and the films produced by Hollywood with so much emphasis on blood and gore, as the heroes blow away thousands in one swipe.

I once saw a nature program that explored the problems faced by young male elephants being raised without a bull elephant. The absence of the bull elephant disrupted the family life of the entire herd. Young male elephants were killing other animals and fighting one another. This went on until an older bull elephant was introduced into the herd. The bull elephant immediately began to control the younger bulls. The killing of other animals and fighting amongst themselves ceased. The older bull represented the balance that was missing.

Human beings also need balance. Absentee fathers represent the same problems, if not worse, for children that the absence of the bull elephant represented for the young bulls. When we accept the fact that children belong to all of us and that every adult should be concerned with every child, we will be able to appreciate why personalizing our relationship with our children is not in our best interest or theirs. When we personalize our relationship with children, we tend to overemphasize everything. We worry about them whenever they are out of sight. We tend to age more quickly and stress ourselves further as a result. The opposite is also a disadvantage. Instead of being there for children we neglect them, never having enough time for them. Between these two extremes is the collective approach, by which a community takes the time necessary to act responsibly toward all children.

Sex

Sex has become a superficial act of affection and serves more as an expression of lust and less as an expression of love. Sex is also used in much the same way as drugs, providing a release or escape from everyday life.

Since men do not understand the relationship between women and themselves, they have not been able to define what their relationship to women should be. One of the results of this lack of understanding is the tension that exists between them when it comes to sex. The lack of understanding is why many women are more interested in a man's financial status rather than the man himself and use sex to achieve their goals of happiness and financial security.

Imagine a little girl growing up and witnessing the bad experiences the mother had with the father, combined with the overall negative interaction with other men in the mother's life. She hears the conversations older female relatives engage in concerning their destructive experiences with men. They also talk to her about how foolish it is for a woman to trust a man or put her faith in a relationship with a man. It is easy to understand why sex would develop into a tool used to create a better life, especially if a young girl's first romantic experience goes bad, as predicted by female friends and family.

Imagine half the little girls in this country having similar experiences. These types of situations will produce a lot of grown women in fifteen or twenty years that will not think of sex as a positive thing.

Little boys grow up witnessing the same experiences regarding the mother and the men in her life. Young and older men tell boys how they get over on women in regards to sex, money and the overall control they exert. It's easy to understand why boys grow up duplicating the same negative actions and attitudes toward women, especially if the men setting these examples are fathers, close relatives, or grown men these little boys look up to. When these little boys grow up, there'll be a lot of grown men who will have no idea how to properly treat women.

Beginning at puberty, most girls, especially the attractive ones, are talked to instead of spoken with. Constantly, young women are picking up signals from men that say, "I want to get into your pants, not your head. I want to enjoy your body, not your mind."

The various games men often play to achieve sexual goals are as varied as the men playing those games. They manipulate women to dress seductively in order to stimulate sexual fantasies, and obviously a large number of women accept this approach to turn men on.

Many men react to almost any woman they see in a sexually seductive outfit while most women only want the men that they find attractive to respond to the way they look. The end result is tension and conflict created between strangers who pass each other in public places because men disrespect the women who don't acknowledge their advances.

The same man, who speaks to a woman when she passes him on the street and calls her names when she doesn't respond, could be the same type of man she meets through friends and family. While a woman is not willing to give this type of man the time of day when he makes advances in public, she appears ready to establish a relationship with him if he is introduced under circumstances considered acceptable.

Women are naturally beautiful, and the ones who don't dress in a seductive way to gain a man's attention are in many ways the most appealing. There are many men who prefer this type of woman because her style and manner stimulates their imaginations more.

It seems that most men are not able to accept marriage vows and often have affairs with other women. Many women rebel against this disrespectful treatment from a significant other and react in the same way. The way that men react to the wives going out with other men has forced women to conceal these activities in the same way men do, and they tend to do a better job at it.

Many men are already suspicious and try to control every move made by the mates because they can't take what they themselves have been dishing out. Women retaliating in response to unacceptable male behavior is not the answer. Women will attract the same types of men as the mates in their because they are doing the same thing that the mates are doing, so the dramatic cycle continues.

Women have justifiably placed a price on sex because men have foolishly made sex more important than the relationship. I don't know any self-respecting woman who would let a man she didn't know into her house without a good reason. And, no self-respecting woman would let a man into her house if she thought he would abuse the privilege. The paradox however, is for a woman to have sex with a man who does not take her well-being into consideration is like letting a stranger into her house who intends to abuse the privilege. She is also giving a man access to her emotions as well as letting him into her body.

Years ago a female friend said, "Women enjoy sex more than men do." I asked her why she thought so. She said, "You go inside of a woman and being inside her is the reason." The answer was like a light being turned on in a dark room. It allowed me to understand why women take longer to agree to sex and why it's that much harder for them to stop once they get started.

A man is considered extremely disrespectful if he enters someone's house and abuses the privilege. Similarly a man commits an offense which violates a woman when he enters her body with the sole intent of satisfying his desire for sex without taking her feelings into consideration. Many men approach women as if women's emotions are not affected by men's selfishness. Without understanding this critical interaction, men lose out on the mutual satisfaction that comes from both partners respecting how each one feels.

In order to break this dramatic cycle men must set positive examples for boys to follow. Teaching young men the connection between what they do and how women respond is the key to correcting the injustices to women, children and themselves.

Observing how women respond helps men to understand what they are doing. Women will not always respond appropriately, but the behavior will indicate the degree of harmony or disharmony when men choose a positive or negative approach to what's being done.

Women and men must re-evaluate the sex games they play because they are games that no one wins. The struggle to gain the upper hand in a relationship is a struggle against the relationship. People can be compared to water and should be accepted at the level they are naturally at without anyone trying to establish control over the other person.

Many women are willing to do without sex before submitting to men who want to control them. They know that these men do not have their interest at heart. Unfortunately, this self-denial of sex is not only unhealthy for the body, but mentally and emotionally unhealthy. Abandoning sex is like abandoning love. Sex with love is the answer, it feeds the soul. Women choose the men in their lives and they should choose men based on how they think instead of how they look, because looks can not sustain a relationship.

Cunnilingus and fellatio are also byproducts of the sex games people play. I don't believe that most women really enjoy fellatio. Young women who still believe in romance might enjoy it. However, I believe more experienced women indulge in fellatio because it is the quickest way to get men to reciprocate. It's like all the other indulgences that society has acquired that result from the imbalance between females and males, which is actually the imbalance inside every one of us.

Since women are not naturally bisexual, why do some women turn to other women for sex? Some say the companionship that is not shared with men and the disharmony existing between women and men when they do establish a relationship, are the main reasons women turn to other women. The friendship women experience with one another, the understanding they share, and the companionship they provide each other while not having a satisfying relationship with a man have all created an environment that can easily become sexual.

The sale of erotic toys, electric and otherwise, that some women use to procure sexual gratification in the absence of a man has become a huge business. The company of men has become so undesirable because of their lack of consideration that women would rather turn to themselves and inanimate objects rather than be with inconsiderate men. Men are also buying sexual toys and rubber dolls for their sexual gratification. The difference is women choose not to deal with men while men have not learned how to properly deal with women. There are also women who are so bitter because of their mistreatment by men that they do what they can to turn other women against men.

Some women become nuns or asexual and devote themselves to the church because they find it difficult to devote themselves to a relationship with a man. There are a number of women who enter the Armed Forces or take up other positions in life that would normally be unacceptable to them for the same reason. They choose to allow their lives to be programmed and orchestrated as an alternative to not finding "the right man" or having a painful relationship with any man.

With all of the challenges and issues women face in a relationship with men can we blame them for being more interested in men who have a lot of money as opposed to someone they can love? Most men have not provided women with the emotional security needed in a relationship so many women continue to look for financial security first.

It's been said that there would be no gay women if there were no gay men. For every action there is an equal and opposite reaction. Men paying less attention to women, men paying more attention to each other and men mistreating women help create the reaction.

Why are there so many gay men in America? Among the situations responsible are: When a boy is raised in a single household with a mother who takes her anger out on her son because of the negative relationship she had with his father; when a boy is raised as a girl by encouraging feminine behavior or being overprotected by his mother; the fact that over two million men are incarcerated and kept from female companionship; male children molested and taken advantage of by adult males; the possibility that fast food and other diets disrupt hormonal balance; the various forms through which homosexuality is promoted in the media, and glamorizing same-sex love are all contributing factors.

By the time girls and boys begin to have romantic interest towards one another, they have inherited a lot of sexual confusion from adults that give rise to questions that they don't have answers to.

Sex is a subject that is often hard for parents to talk about with children because our society is so repressed when it comes to dealing with sex and the human body. A young woman is in the first stage of womanhood when she first gets her period. Her hormones are asking for attention. Boys begin to take on a greater significance. She thinks she is ready for sex and physically she is. However, mentally she needs a mother's help, and mother should be willing to talk with her about the young man she wants to spend time with. A mother giving her opinion about the daughter's date helps them both learn and grow together. Most young women never get this kind of support and guidance from parents. This lack of support is part of the reason why we are in such a dire situation.

At this time in a young woman's life, young men of the same age are thinking like boys. They will say and do almost anything to have sex with young women. While most young women are looking for romance and boyfriends, most young men are looking for sex and fun. So in order to get young men to pay more attention and spend more time with them, women are likely to use sex as an expedient for negotiating the relationship. It's like using a carrot in front of a donkey to get the donkey to pull the wagon.

When a young woman is satisfied that the boy is interested in her, she is ready to have sex with him. This approach is doomed from the start because young men play the sex game too well. At this point boys will give girls more attention and more time. They might even stop hanging out with their friends because they are busy trying to "get over."

After the novelty of having sex has worn off, young men eventually return to friends, sports and hanging out. Girls begin to feel as if they were taken advantage of. Some girls withdraw, some chase and follow after these boys, while some rebel, argue and fight with them. A girl's first romance can be a rude awakening because young men are not usually prepared to be in a serious relationship.

As a mother attempts to come to the daughter's aid, she should keep in mind that this is all new to the daughter. She may not want the mother to help guide her. At this point a mother's patience and understanding is vital. It is important for a mother to be there for the daughter if she accepts her help and, at the same time allow her daughter the freedom to learn on her own if she doesn't want the mother's help. If things don't work out, this approach helps the daughter to be more receptive in the future.

When a mother sits down to talk with the teenage daughter, there is much to consider. She has not had enough experience with boys in order to take any of them seriously. She has her whole life ahead of her and needs to get an independent sense of herself. After a mother helps to educate the daughter, there are times when it may be all right to have sex after talking it through with her mother.

People are aware that there are fathers who pay for their son's first sexual experience upon reaching sexual maturity. There are also mothers who introduce their daughters to men they trust to have their first sexual experience with because of the drama that they know young men subject young women to.

There are boys who will like and respect the daughter. If the daughter in turn likes one of them enough to have sex with him, she should be prepared to go back to being with friends without feeling hurt if the boy is not ready for a relationship. When she is able to do this, she will stand out among friends and among boys. The friends will seek her advice and look up to her. The boys will respect and want to be around her. She must be secure enough with herself to accept that she has a right to a physical release as much as the boy does. If the boy turns out to be a jerk, her spirit will not be broken and she will not feel as if she is being used. She is learning to know which boys to stay away from. Through experience she will slowly be able to recognize a man who has matured and developed enough of his own qualities that help to make him a responsible person.

A relationship has a slim chance of success if sex is used as a tool to catch a male, or to keep one in line. When the novelty of the sex act wears off, there's not much left if there is no emotional or intellectual appreciation of each other.

When girls and boys start school, they naturally become attracted to one another. We grow up believing that dating someone of the same age is what we are supposed to do. Same age relationships between females and males for the most part do not work. Most eastern cultures recognize this. Moslem males are taught to approach women at 15 years of age when they are 23 years old. Various African and Asian cultures are taught that the woman should be half the man's age plus seven (if he's 26, she should be 13 + 7 = 20). Of course, age balance does not guarantee a successful relationship if a man has not been taught the importance of being responsible. Thus our romantic and sexual cultural conditioning leaves a lot to be desired because we have not made age difference or responsibility the important subjects that they are.

Drugs have also played an important part in sexuality. Street drugs, over-the-counter pharmaceutical drugs, and chemicals in our food have heightened and stimulated the sex drive as well as affected the nervous system. All drugs have a negative effect on the nervous system. In the short run we are more stimulated sexually. In the long run we alter and destroy the longevity of sexuality.

The drugs and chemicals that we have accepted into our bodies are also passed down to the unborn children through the sperm and egg cells that form the embryo. Many mental, emotional and physical defects in newborn babies also result as much from the drugs and chemicals that parents pass on to babies as they do from other imbalances that exist in our chemical makeup.

There are women who would make great mothers but choose not to have children because they have not found the right mate. They voluntarily give up their natural birthright to bear children. They would rather go through life never knowing what it's like to give birth. Then there are women who settle on having a baby without carefully choosing the man because the desire to give birth is so strong. They are often prepared to raise the child alone.

Since the choice of a man is up to the woman, she should be encouraged and taught to take her time and choose carefully. If she rushes to make the choice, she is gambling with her right to happiness. If she chooses to use her body instead of her mind, she will attract men who will not be prepared to stay with her, given that the men she attracts will respond to how she presents herself.

We should all begin to think about the results of the sex games we play on each other and ourselves.

Drugs

In the 1960s much was said about the culture in the United States becoming a drug culture. It has now become as automatic to pop a pill and take a spoon full of chemicals as it is to have something to eat and drink. The food, water and air contain enough chemicals to seem more like drugs than nature's gifts.

There are pharmaceutical drugs or chemicals in almost everything we consume. Because of all the chemicals put into the food we eat, it is virtually impossible to know what the food naturally tastes like.

Americans are able to buy more drugs than other world citizens because of their greater wealth. The U.S.A. represents roughly 4.5% of the world's population,[2] yet we consume 67% of the world's illegal

---

[2] Wikipedia: U.S. Census Bureau, Demographics of the United States; census.gov/main/www/popclock.html

drugs. This is a staggering percentage of drugs consumed by so few people. It means that we are more doped up than the rest of the world and therefore suffer more from the harmful effects of drugs. When we add legal drugs to this scenario, it's easy to understand why people are not walking around in a normal frame of mind.

The public is constantly being given information about broken marriages, battered women, abused children, murders and suicides that are all caused by street drugs. What is not being told are the similar dangers of pharmaceutical drugs and chemicals put into our food and drinks. If people are given the correct information concerning the destructive nature of these chemicals, many of us might stop using pharmaceutical drugs. Imagine learning that what is supposed to cure you is actually helping to make the problem worse than it is.

All drugs directly attack the central nervous system in an all-out assault. The central nervous system determines who we are, what we say and do and how we react to what other people say and do. Drugs destroy the nerve endings and we lose a little bit of ourselves each time we use drugs. Have you ever left one room to go into another room to get something and by the time you got there, you forgot what you wanted to get? This happens to many people regardless of age because of the drugs and chemicals interfering with the brains' ability to function properly.

In August of 2004, a radio report stated that 200,000 people die every year from over-the-counter pharmaceutical drugs. Far fewer people die every year due to street drug consumption than from pharmaceutical drugs. Does this mean that street drugs are less harmful? It's telling us that pharmaceutical drugs are taken by far more people because they can be obtained legally. More people drink alcohol for the same reason; it's legal.

Pharmaceutical drugs in the body affect us in the same way that street drugs do. They distort perception, make us anxious or sluggish and destroy our mental and physical health. Decision-making is impaired and the memory becomes faulty because drugs slowly eat away the brain cells. With street drugs, these effects are immediate because they are more concentrated and powerful. With pharmaceutical drugs and chemicals in medicine and food, the process takes a little longer, but the effects are the same.

Doctors let us know that we may have side effects from the drugs that they prescribe. Many times the side effects are worse than the original ailment. This fact alone should tell us that something is clearly wrong with prescription drugs. There is also something wrong with people (Doctors and Pharmacist) who claim to cure us by prescribing a drug that helps us trade one illness for another. There is also something wrong with those of us who accept this kind of a treatment. Getting back in touch with nature is the answer to curing our health challenges.

Unfortunately drugs are more harmful to women and children. Women are the bearers of life and more intricately put together which makes them more susceptible to drugs and children's bodies are not strong enough to handle the chemicals in drugs.

A multi-billion-dollar economy has been created from the sale of legal and illegal drugs. Professionals quickly prescribe drugs instead of focusing on the natural way in which to cure what ails us. The public must accept the blame for this because we accept the use of drugs without question.

Some years ago, a number of people died from taking an-over the-counter pharmaceutical drug. This information was channeled to the public by the media. The manufacturers recalled the drugs. Two months later the drugs were back on store shelves, and it was business as usual. Sales returned to where they were before the deaths. It was as if the incidents never happened. Are we that gullible? Is television and advertising that powerful? Why are we willing to act like robots regardless of the consequences?

We often hear about drug-related horror stories including husbands murdering wives, wives murdering husbands, children murdering parents, and parents murdering children. These acts have increased to the same degree that our drug consumption has increased.

The pharmaceutical drug industry has now set its focus on children as its latest target audience. The problem has become so out of control that the Citizen's Commission on Human Rights publishes a booklet called *Psychiatry, Betraying and Drugging Children*, to warn people. It is devoted entirely to discussing the dangers of psychiatrists' administering drugs to children and how these drugs are creating zombies.

Drugs are being given to children without any concern for the emotional and neurological problems they cause. With the help of the Psychiatry-Psychiatric Committee for the Welfare and Protection of Children, parents have united to officially testify to the harmful effects of these drugs.

It is widely acknowledged that today's youth are in a very destructive frame of mind. This fact has a lot to do with drugs already flowing through their veins at the time of their birth. Far too many of the parents were taking drugs in one form or another. This is one of the reasons previously unheard-of acts of violence by children against adults and other children have been perpetrated. The time bomb had been ticking for years. What should now concern us are the solutions needed to resolve these issues.

There are numerous ways we can help children understand the harmful effects from taking drugs. Visit rehabilitation centers to talk with recovering addicts. Go on field trips to prisons, and let the prisoners talk about the loss of freedom because of drugs. Form discussion groups so children can talk with each other about drugs. These actions will help teach children more effectively than a commercial on television or what they can read in a book.

When we accept drugs, we exclude people, places and things. We lose people who are close to us because they don't want to be around and watch us destroy ourselves. Those friends and relatives who do stand by us are usually subjected to painful experiences. Consider the accidental deaths that are the result of violent and non-violent situations that could have been prevented if not for the use of drugs.

When someone is arrested for street drugs, the resulting problems can totally disrupt their life. There may be legal fees and a police record that follows one for life. There may also have to be time spent in a rehabilitation center. Unless the individual has the discipline to stay away from drugs without going to a treatment center, he or she winds up taking a legal drug as a substitute for a street drug. Some people find themselves going to counseling sessions for years before they are free of either drug.

The sale of illegal drugs is reported to be well over 80 billion dollars a year. This is why the competition among dealers is so fierce. Drug dealers are competing for the same drug dollars without any regard for human life. Reading the daily papers about a drug war or killing is a daily occurrence. Too often the children of drug dealers have been murdered because the parents could not protect themselves or the children against the dangers of the drug world.

Once upon a time many people thought that drug dealers came from impoverished families. More so now than ever before, middle class and upper class people are getting involved in the illegal drug trade. It seems that the flamboyant life style and mesmerizing attention that drug dealers receive is part of the reason. The danger, the partying and the money seem to send a message that says a boring 9-to-5 job or running a family business is not as lucrative or exciting as the illegal drug business.

A detective friend of mine once said, "With the exception of organized crime and the very rich that are protected by power and wealth, the average drug dealer last approximately three to five years. They either wind up being killed, jailed or on public assistance."

Imagine youngsters growing into adults, in a world surrounded by drugs. With all the other problems they face, how can they eventually find love and happiness with a potential soul mate while all drugged up? It is almost impossible. The use of drugs has a lot to do with why many married couples get divorced.

Imagine discovering things that you like about someone while you are high on drugs. Imagine not liking those same things about that person when you are sober. You argue and fight and nothing seems right, so you get drugged up again. But you can't stay high all day, every day. It is only when you become clean and free of drugs that you can begin to see things clearly. It could take years before two people realize that they were not meant to be together. Thus, two people go their separate ways after spending so much time trying to make a relationship work based on drugs.

The statistics on divorce are much higher than reported because they do not include the people who separate without a legal divorce, or the couples who don't get legally married and separate after years of living together.

When you are on drugs, your perception is faulty, your understanding is deceptive, and your ability to think is flawed. In other words, you are not in your natural frame of mind. You also become a slave to whatever drug you are taking. You repeatedly go through the process of getting high and coming down.

I knew a couple who were greatly affected by the street drugs they consumed. After they had been doing drugs for a year, I became convinced that they were no longer the same people that I knew. They were always high and always arguing about something. The drugs had altered their perception of reality. He became jealous of her every move and she became suspicious of his. At first, they would apologize for their actions. Later on the apologies stopped as the problems grew worse. Eventually they both signed themselves into a rehabilitation center.

I also observed the effect of drugs on a friend I use to socialize with. When he was high, he was the life of the party. You could not find a friendlier person to be around. He was the perfect gentleman with women, and most of them wanted to share time with him. When he became sober, he was just the opposite: quiet, withdrawn and moody. You would be lucky to get two words out of him. He avoided being around people when he was sober and eventually developed a liver and kidney problem. He reluctantly entered a drug-counseling program to solve his problem. Unfortunately, not much could be done for his kidney or liver disease.

I have a friend that comes by my place every now and then to ask my advice about different things. On one particular occasion he mentioned that for years his drug of choice was cocaine. He is a very handsome guy with a girlfriend who has never indulged in drugs. He claims the girlfriend accepted his drug habit because it did not have any effect on their lifestyle.

He said that back in 1987 he began free-basing. He said that when he was sniffing cocaine, he could stay at a party and continue to dance or socialize without any problem. However, when he started free-basing, (or smoking cocaine) his whole lifestyle slowly began to change. He could not stay at a party and dance or socialize because he preferred to be with other crack users. Crack is the name used to describe cocaine smoking when the cocaine is purchased already prepared for people to smoke. He was always late for work and he could no longer save money. His health began to fail, and his girlfriend eventually left him.

Before he started smoking cocaine, he would sniff it wearing his suit and tie. Now when he came home from work he would change into his dungarees and sneakers and go into the most dangerous neighborhoods in order to buy his drugs. He said he would stay in those neighborhoods to continue getting high. He stated that his biggest surprise was how his standard in women had changed.

He explained that while under the influence of the drug, he would approach women that he never would have spoken to while sober. Finally, he told me that when he lost his job, the mother had banned him from seeing the daughter. He came to his senses and quit cold turkey and has remained sober ever since.

It's been said that most of the drug users in life are people who do not care about anything but themselves. They do not seem to appreciate family ties, or feel responsible to other family members. When the family structure is not stable, drugs make an already bad situation worse.

When you consider the vast amount of drugs brought into this country and the crime that the drug business is inflicting upon society, it is clear that we have not addressed the drug problem responsibly. If you don't want someone bringing an unwanted item into the home, you don't let them in. If we really did not want people importing illegal drugs into this country, we could put a stop to it.

Research and tests have substantiated that the average human being thinks 30 to 35 thousand thoughts a day. Sixty percent of those thoughts are classified as negative; 35% of those thoughts are classified as useless, for example (what kind of lipstick should I put on or what tie should I wear); and 5% of those thoughts are classified as positive. If only 5% of an average person's thoughts are positive, it's easy to understand why so many people turn to drugs and stay on drugs for a long period of time.

In order to become a healthy society, we must think with a healthy mindset housed in a healthy body. Schools need to find an effective way to teach children the dangers of taking drugs. Even though children are taught anatomy, physiology and physical education from the early grades into high school, people continue to damage their bodies by taking drugs.

We have created the greatest drug culture in history. How is it possible to cultivate successful relationships with anyone while all drugged up?

Food

We are all products of our biology, our environment and our culture. How we are raised and what we are taught determines to a large extent the goals we will achieve and the road we will walk. The food we eat is also a result of the environment and culture. You are what you eat is more than just a philosophical phrase, it is a fact.

People eat differently all over the world. Some of what they eat is good and wholesome, but the vast majority of what people eat is unhealthy. Americans, having more money to spend than most people around the world, buy and consume more food that diminishes health and well being than any other group of people in the world. As a consequence, they find themselves suffering more from obesity and serious diseases than other people. How can you expect to have and maintain a healthy relationship with your mate or anyone if you are not healthy?

Over time the concept and perception of how and why we eat has changed. Today we eat for taste and not for health. As a result, we are reducing the length and quality of our lives. We have strayed so far from the natural, healthful way of eating that we see the unnatural foods and habits and the results from them as normal. If we don't change our eating habits, it will be difficult for our children to change theirs, and this trend will continue into future generations.

The above is paraphrased from a letter to parents on the back cover of the award winning *The Children's Health Food Book*. I wrote the book for children and their parents in the sincere hope that dialogue and reinforcement around proper nutrition could be established between them.

Many diseases result from what we put into our bodies, what our parents put into their bodies or what their parents had put into their bodies. Poor health and disease are passed on through each generation, as genetic makeup gets weaker and weaker from unhealthy eating habits. We can go all the way back up the family tree to get a better understanding of this problem. Many people believe they inherited diseases from parents. In the majority of such cases, what they have inherited is the same diet, which resulted in the same diseases as the parents.

If you ate the same food as your parents and your parents ate the same food as their parents, there is a good chance the disease from that diet is going to be the same for everyone.

Why is it that the U.S.A. can feed the rest of the world many times over and even have a food surplus, yet there are countries that cannot go an entire year without having to worry about the devastation of starvation? We now have the technology to create genetically engineered and hybridized food, both plant and animal. Cross breeding plants with other plant species are responsible for what we commonly know as genetically engineered or hybridized food.

Both genetically engineered and hybridized foods were created for the purpose of allowing a plant to survive under conditions that normally would destroy it. For example, by grafting a cold weather plant with a warm weather plant, the warm weather plant can now thrive in cold weather. Seventy percent of all soy foods are genetically engineered, as are the vast majority of tomatoes and potatoes.[3] Unfortunately, there are no laws that require that such foods be labeled to indicate if they are products of genetic engineering or not. In the final analysis, neither genetically engineered nor hybridized food will nourish the body. This being the case, we should concern ourselves with the long-term effects of these foods on our bodies and on our overall health! We should be asking what we could do to stop this practice, which seems to be motivated more by the desire for profits than for improving the quality of life.

Humans will never be able to improve on food that is naturally created. Food the Creator has given us to sustain life, is mostly alkaline. Anything man has tampered with becomes acidic in its composition. Acid erodes and eats away at the substances it comes in contact with, including the body. Within the health community it's said that our overall food consumption should be 80% alkaline and 20% acid. Unfortunately, most of our food intake is more like the reverse – 80% acid and 20% alkaline. This is why many of us are

---

[3] The Campaign: Grassroots Political Action, thecampaign.org

prone to disease – the acid based foods that we eat are slowly eating us up from the inside out.

Our bodies can turn anything we eat into fuel. Just like the railroad engines of the Old West in the 1800's, you could throw anything that would burn into the furnace to supply power in order to drive the train. Certain types of fuel were more efficient, yielding longer burns and supplying more power per weight than other kinds. But a prolonged use of any fuel that was not designed for the furnace would soon hurt the engine and shorten its lifespan. It is exactly the same with humans. Food not designed for the body, while allowing us to sustain life, will eventually hurt us and shorten life.

Whether we realize it or not, we are in a very dangerous situation. We run the risk of having all of the food we eat provided by large genetic engineering conglomerates instead of farmers who grow the food on farmland. Soon those two words "farmer" and "farmland" may very well be spoken of as relics from a distant past. This is because there are those who stubbornly insist on improving or conquering nature, rather than working and living in harmony with nature.

However, the increase in debilitating diseases and the decrease in the quality of health dictate that now is the time to find the way back to nature and natural foods.

Babies are dying at an alarming rate because mothers are made to believe that formulas sold over the counter are nutritious as or even more nutritious than breast milk. Breast milk strengthens a baby's immune system. Without breast-feeding, the rashes, colds and fevers that babies get have a greater chance of becoming serious health problems. The term "crib death" has been used to describe some kind of mystery or unexplainable phenomenon. Are the cribs responsible for the deaths of so many babies? If we keep your babies out of the cribs, would there be no babies dying? Newborn babies need breast milk to build and maintain a strong immune system. A strong immune system will protect babies against life-threatening diseases. Babies also need to sleep with mothers, not in a crib.

The Creator gave mothers the ability to produce milk in their breasts for a few reasons. One is to feed and nourish their precious babies, despite the schemes of business-minded men who produce, market and sell baby formulas! Though not emphasized enough, the emotional bonding shared between a mother and child comes from breast feeding. The better the quality of food eaten, the better the quality of breast milk produced. This is one reason why mothers and mothers-to-be should focus as much on the natural way of eating as possible. Even if you do not desire motherhood, staying in good health is a good thing.

If food is not natural, it is unnatural. If it is unnatural, it is not good you. If it is not good for you, it will not be good for children.

Women and children are not responsible for the way big business has controlled and manipulated the food industry. However, women can play a pivotal role in assuring that only the best quality food is made available to us all. Women who understand the connection between proper nutrition and the health of children and themselves can accomplish this by following a few simple steps.

The first step is to get information from books on food and nutrition that can be purchased at most health food stores. *Become Younger* by Dr. Norman Walker, *Survival Into the 21st Century* by Victoras

Kulvinskas, *Mucusless Diet Healing System* by Arnold Ehret, *Raw Soul, Health Journey* by Lillian Butler & Eddie Robinson, and *Raw Power* by Stephin Arlin are five excellent books to start with.

The second step is to share the information with as many people as possible. Talk with family, friends and associates to help them understand how important proper nutrition is to a healthy survival.

The third step is to make changes in your own life. There's nothing like feeling the results for yourself. For example, have fruit for breakfast instead of eggs, bacon or pastry. Rather than coffee, try an herbal tea for that morning pep. Fresh-squeezed orange or grapefruit juice is excellent! At lunchtime, try eating more salads with your meals. You might even want to include some vegetable juice as well. Finally, at dinnertime, try cutting out the pastries for dessert, and have a nice fruit-bowl instead. You will be happily surprised with the results.

The fourth step, which actually is fused with the third, is to buy the healthiest foods possible. Buy organic. Patronize those companies that are committed to providing the best in quality and nutrition. When you make the decision to change how you shop and eat, the corporations, no matter how big they are, will make the decision to change what they provide.

There are public announcements on television that suggest that we can "just say no" to drugs. If we substitute bad food for drugs, we will still be in the dilemma where we might say no vocally, but still be unable to stop without the proper knowledge and information. You must have or develop the infrastructure to use the information you do get in order to maintain Discipline and Will Power. Reading will give you that support. You will not be able to just say no to anything that you want to do without knowledge about it. You must network with other like-minded people to help strengthen your resolve.

Many supermarket chains around the country now have special sections where you can purchase health food products that are normally sold in health food stores. Why the shift? Even more so, why have people been buying at health food stores? The answer is simple, the desires to get organic produce – food produced without synthetic chemicals is growing as people become more educated.

Organic produce is a multi-billion dollar market that is increasing at eight times the rate of the packaged food business. Packaged Facts estimates that 2008 sales of natural and organic food and beverages will continue at a double-digit growth rate to reach $32.9 billion.[4] The big corporations are starting to meet the demands of an educated and health-conscious public.

The food most of us eat contains so many chemicals that we are really unable to appreciate the taste of real food. These chemicals are having a negative effect on the brain's ability to function. One of these chemicals, monosodium glutamate, also known as MSG, slowly eats away the brain cells. Some of us are forgetful and sluggish without realizing it's the drugs and chemicals in the food we have eaten that make us feel and act this way. This "chemical confusion" sometimes causes people to say or do things that we later regret. We are not as aware of how drugs and chemicals in the food affect behavior as we are about street drugs, such as crack, cocaine or heroin. Street drugs have more of an immediate effect on us, while

---

[4] AFN Thought For Food: Surge in natural and organic food a billion dollar boom that just might last, September 10, 2008, Daniel Palmer

the drugs and chemicals in our food take much longer to affect us. The impact is subtle but in the long run just as profound. Our behavior is moody, the confusion and forgetfulness are long term, and the diseases that result, if not checked, are devastating.

Man is naturally a vegetarian, and many animals are also. Those animals that are natural carnivores and people who eat meat require more oxygen. The higher oxygen intake speeds up breathing, the heartbeat and all of our bodily functions. This is one of the reasons why meat eaters don't live as long as vegetarians. Vegetarians require less oxygen, and this decreased amount slows down breathing and the aging process, as the body's systems are not being overworked. The quicker the motion of any machine, the sooner it will wear out. Rabbits live a few years because they take quick short breaths, move around very quickly and their heartbeats are rapid. Turtles live over a hundred years because they breathe and move slowly, and have slow heartbeats. Maybe we should all learn from the turtle.

According to Dr. Richard Schulze, a renowned herbalist and natural health advocate, meat eating causes more deaths than anything else does. He says,

"Add up all of the causes of death, airplane crashes, auto accidents, poisoning, drowning, suicides, electrocutions, sky diving, drug overdoses, street drugs, murders, violent crimes, AIDS, cancer and every other disease, add them all up and they don't even come close to how many people die each year from heart attacks and strokes." He adds that, "One million people die each year from the cholesterol and fat from the animals that they ate, which are clogging up the heart or coronary arteries or brain or cerebral arteries that supply blood to the internal organs. When the blood supply is blocked, the organs die and we die."

There is a divine balance of law and order, of cause and effect, with the Universe. When we kill animals with all kinds of weapons from the outside, they will kill us with all kinds of diseases from the inside. Whenever any one person or group of people abuse their power and control over other people, other creatures or other things, there is always going to be a price to pay. We cannot escape the negative karma that results from killing animals.

Meat is considered the worst of the bad foods. However, sweets are just as damaging to the body because people eat sweets about ten times a day while only eating meat two or three times a day. The vast majority of Americans have a love affair with sweets of some kind. In whatever sweets people buy, sugar will be the sweetener used the majority of times. It is the constant intake of sugar that makes its effects on people as damaging as meat.

Sugar is responsible for sugar diabetes, bad teeth, diseased pancreas and kidney failure. Sugar also helps to cause constipation; it robs the body of multi-vitamins and makes children and adults more irritable and neurotic. These are just some of the ills of sugar.

Processed starch is just as bad as sugar and maybe worse, again, because of how often we eat it. People eat so much starchy foods that our bodies crave it when we try to stop. I have heard many people testify to not being able to do without starch in the same way people speak about not being able to do without cigarettes or coffee. Be mindful that starch also turns into sugar inside of our bodies.

Processed starch contains carbonic acid, which can make the liver as hard as a piece of wood. After the heart, the liver is the most important organ in the body.

Processed starch speeds up the aging process quicker than any other food because it dries you out. It is a cause of stones in the gall bladder and the kidneys, and is greatly responsible for hemorrhoids, tumors, cancer and many other problems.

We should also avoid dairy foods; they release too much lactic acid in the body. Butter, cheese, milk, yogurt and ice cream are just a few of the dairy products that create lactic acid. Dairy products cause cholesterol to form in the arteries, and help to create high blood pressure and poor blood circulation. Dairy products also contain casein – a substance used to make cement.

When digested by the body, all of the above foods turn into mucus. Mucus moves through our body's many systems like mud, choking off our oxygen supplies. Again, herein lies the source of our dietary health problems – the lack of oxygen assimilation. Our food should move through our bodies more like water, not like mud. When it moves through our bodies like water, we stay healthier and live longer. This happens when we make fruits, vegetables, whole grains (soaked overnight and eaten raw) and sea vegetables our main diet. These are the ideal foods for us to eat. They come directly from nature, grown on a tree, a vine, or from the sea. Vegetables, fruits, natural grains and sea vegetables receive the ultraviolet rays from the sun which are necessary to sustain life, energize our bodies and give us strength. Without the sunlight all living creatures on earth would die. Man-made processed food that comes in a can, a carton or a box is detrimental to our health because it is full of mucus. This food will fill us up and make us fat, but it will not give us the necessary minerals, vitamins or nutrients that we need for optimum health.

Vegetables, fruits, natural grains and sea vegetables are light, live wholesome foods. These foods will easily move through our body's system, and not wear us out and make us tired as heavy foods do. These foods also contain oxygen, and when we consume these foods we automatically become stronger, healthier and are able to resist illnesses. Notice that after a heavy processed lunch, employees are lethargic and perform less efficiently.

According to the New York Post, (May 10, 2000), Lance Armstrong, the Tour de France champ who battled back from a near fatal cancer to win the world's most grueling bike race in 1999, said that cancer was the best thing that ever happened to him... "There is no question in my mind that I would never have won the Tour de France if I hadn't gotten cancer."

In 1996, at age 25, he found out he had testicular cancer, and that the tumors had spread to his lungs and brain. "I underwent brain surgery, removal of a testicle and rigorous chemotherapy treatment during which I lost 20 pounds and every muscle I had ever built up."

Armstrong said that while he knew he had won the war against cancer, he had been traumatized by the battle. He gave up riding and became a bum.

"I played golf every day, I water-skied, I drank beer, and I lay on the sofa and channel-surfed."

He said his fiancée snapped him out of it, telling him, "You need to decide if you are going to retire for real and be a golf-playing, beer-drinking, Mexican-food-eating slob." "I started riding again a week later."

As he began rigorous training for the 1999 Tour de France, Armstrong said he noticed one unforeseen benefit of cancer... "It had completely reshaped my body. I was leaner in body and more balanced in spirit."

I found this story fascinating and inspiring for a number of reasons. First, it shows how devastating cancer can be on our overall health as a result of bad food. Second, he tells us that he was traumatized by the battle to survive the cancer treatment. Most of the people who more often survive surgery, radiation and chemotherapy treatments are athletes and the young. The average person has not built up their bodies to the extent that they can withstand the trauma of traditional modern cancer treatments; old people are no longer strong enough. Third, he talks about the unforeseen benefit of cancer. Note, he says, "I was leaner in body and more balanced in spirit." This revelation is what should concern us most. He lost weight and it affected him spiritually. Historians have reported that the majority of geniuses throughout the world are born during hard times and times of famine.

How can we get closer to the Creator while constantly stuffing our bodies with food? How can we find our true selves or true love while killing and eating other living creatures for the sake of our taste buds?

Our sense of spirituality is going to be lacking, and we will suffer physically and emotionally. It's like static in a radio. The food blocks our spiritual connection to the Creator and those we love just as static from a radio blocks our reception. The food we eat is full of chemicals, hybrid, synthetic, and a poor substitute for the beneficial foods we can eat.

Now in the 21st century, we should strive to get back to nature, at least as far as food is concerned. If we do not solve our food and eating crises, we will remain a diseased society, giving birth to generations of sickly people.

Women having miscarriages and needing cesarean births are becoming more and more common. Miscarriages are following the path of the food we eat. As the food has become progressively worse over the years, miscarriages and cesarean births have occurred more frequently.

Whenever a woman miscarries, all eyes seem to focus on her and her deficiencies; no one considers the possible role of the man with whom she has conceived the child. Men must also share some of the blame and burden in this life giving process.

We should remember that our bodies convert the food that we eat into blood cells, organs, bone tissue and everything that the human body is made of. How can man's sperm cells be in optimal health, when they themselves are a product of hamburgers, French fries, pancakes, eggs, cheese, candy, coffee, milk, pizza, hot dogs, pastries, pork chops, spare ribs, meat loaf, ice cream, peanut butter and jelly sandwiches, or any of the many fast foods we eat today? It's the same as putting a bad seed into the ground trying to grow a healthy plant. It will not happen. The seed and the soil must be grade "A" quality in order for the plant to be healthy.

Women have been gifted with enough eggs in their ovaries to conceive right up until the time they are eighty to ninety years old. The Hunza women are living examples of this. Their excellent health is attributed to the pure air they breathe, the mineral-rich water they drink, and the fact that much of their diet consists of live food. Thus, their internal and reproductive organs are in tune with nature; they are not clogged up or broken down and diseased.

Why are women in more "advanced" societies unable to conceive once they reach their fifties? Simple, their reproductive organs are clogged with mucus from the processed "improved" food. On rare occasions some women give birth in their fifties, and usually only after taking fertility drugs.

The Hunzas live in the Himalayan Mountains near Mongolia. Why not visit a health food store and inquire about a book on these unique people to learn more about them and their "secrets" to a long and quality life?

I attended a health seminar in 1996, and had the opportunity to meet a woman in her nineties. As we talked, her message was simple. "If you want to live, eat live food; if you want to die, eat dead food."

Though I already had this kind information, the simplicity of the statement hit home and became my advice to everyone I talk to about food.

In the beginning, there was no cooking. We picked our food from a tree or a vine, or it dropped to the ground, and then we ate it. Diseases started with cooking and processing food. Anything you cook, you kill. It doesn't matter if it is fruit, vegetable or animal. Cooking destroys enzymes, nutrients and vitamins. Cooking food is the same as processing food. In either case, you end up with the same thing – dead food. Processed foods are also addictive. Part of the reason for this is that, being generally bland, processed foods need seasoning. For the most part, seasoning stimulates the taste buds, which usually leads to overeating and in many cases becoming overweight. It is generally accepted that people who are overweight tend to be more prone to disease and ill health.

Psychiatrists should start to factor in their patient's diet when prescribing and administering medication. Not just patients who have eating disorders, but any patient that eats the Standard American Diet (SAD). If we are not eating organic uncooked fruits, vegetables, sea vegetables or whole grains, our brainpower is being greatly affected. Prolonged eating of the wrong foods is a factor in mental disorders, such as senility, Alzheimer's, depression and schizophrenia. If we are not healthy, we can not create long lasting relationships with our mates.

Very sick people are being operated on and dying on the operating table. Results like this should not surprise anyone. A very sick person is not supposed to have the strength to survive a major operation. This is the reason you hear something like, "The operation was a success, but the patient died."

We treat very sick people with atomic radiation and chemotherapy. In many cases their hair falls out, their skin changes color, and they lose a lot of weight. There is something wrong with treatment of this kind. We suffer and lose our lives for the sake of our taste buds because we don't eat live wholesome food. This is why we must read the right books, and give ourselves the option to choose the road we want to walk. We must also pass this knowledge on to children. Children will most likely acquire the same diseases that we developed, but if we give them the knowledge, they will feed their children the natural alternative way because they were aware and understood that they inherited our diseases because they ate the same food we ate.

At this point I would like to acknowledge my gratitude to Dr. Norman W. Walker, a health food pioneer who opened my eyes and had a profound effect on my decision to change my diet.

When I was in college, I was in and out of health food stores buying most of the health books on proper diet. When I purchased and read *"Become Younger"* by Dr. Walker, I was so impressed with the book that I called the publishers to find out how I could get in touch with the author. They were receptive. I called Dr. Walker and introduced myself as a student who had read his book and was so moved by the information that I just had to speak with him. He told me he was working in his laboratory and could only give me five minutes of his time. I was surprised at how sharp his voice was and how alert he appeared to be. We wound up speaking for forty minutes. In his book *"Become Younger"* Dr Walker states that whenever people ask him his age he would always tell them he was ageless and so were they. I was surprised and felt privileged when he told me how old he was. By the end of the conversation, I told him how honored I was to have spoken with him and I hoped he lived another 116 years. He responded by telling me he probably would. "You're joking of course." "No I'm not. Have you ever heard of Li-Ching Yun?" "No I haven't, who's he?" "Li-Ching Yun was a Chinese man who lived to be 256 years old. He died in 1933."

I found this information astounding. Over the years I have read books that referred to Li-Ching Yun. When he reached 150 years of age, the Chinese Government celebrated his birthday. When he reached his 200th birthday, people from all over the world went to China to document his age and bear witness to his phenomenal story. During this particular time, he gave three reasons for his longevity. Every day he would walk five miles to teach at the University and five miles back home. He didn't eat food that didn't receive the ultra violet rays from the sun, and he did not worry about anything. The 1937 movie "Lost Horizon" starring Ronald Coleman was inspired by Li-Ching Yun's life.

I consider myself fortunate to have spoken with Dr. Walker four more times before he left the planet. I would buy copies of *"Become Younger,"* give the book to friends and tell them if they read the book and want to keep it, send me the money or return the book.

I believe Dr. Walker lived 10 more years.

In 1987, I had found out from a friend that Dr. John Henrik Clarke, the esteemed historian, was going blind. I managed to procure Dr. Clarke's phone number and called him. I first introduced myself as one who had the greatest admiration for the work he had done. Then I proceeded to ask him about the reports of his impending blindness. He confirmed the reports and said he had been operated on six months prior to my call. I was dismayed because I had hoped to refer him to a number of herbalists and natural doctors who had a track record in successfully treating a number of diseases with herbs and proper diet. Unfortunately, the operation closed the door to any possibility of restoring his eyesight. The operation had severed the lifeline to his eyes. When the lifeline to any of your organs has been cut, the process of cleaning the organs of toxic matter and rebuilding them with proper herbs and diet cannot be accomplished. When I look back, I wonder if he would have been receptive to the natural approach because many people I knew were not.

In yet another situation, a friend told me about a neighbor who was about to have brain surgery, in 1993. After getting some information about the neighbor, I asked if I could go to the hospital the next time she went so that I could talk with the neighbor about alternative treatment. She thought it was a good idea and agreed to let me come with her.

I went to the hospital and met this very sweet and friendly young woman. Using as much diplomacy and tact as possible, I told her about the use of herbs and proper diet to cleanse her body and build it back to good health. I suggested that she could always reschedule the operation if the natural approach did not work. She eventually decided to have the brain surgery and wound up needing a second surgery. After the two operations, her speech became impaired, and she lost coordination on one side of her face.

Some vegetarians die at a young age from some of the same diseases that most meat eaters die from. It could be that they are among those vegetarians who eat as much or perhaps more processed starch, sweets, and cooked processed food that many meat eaters do. Dropping meat from your diet is the right approach to staying healthy but it is not a panacea by itself. Eating the right foods and learning which foods are best for you helps to complete the process, as well as clean water, air, a positive state of mind and exercise.

I often hear, "We're going to die anyway, so why not eat what you want to eat and enjoy life?"

True, we all are going to die, but when you think of the misery and disease associated with this desire to "enjoy" life, it turns out to be more like misery than joy. It would be a miserable existence to live 30 – 40 years with ill health.

We must consider the quality of life. If we can forego the illusion of temporary enjoyment, we will have real enjoyment in the years to come with a healthy body and a sound mind.

How serious are health problems such as cancer, fibroid tumors, high blood pressure, sugar diabetes, asthma, appendicitis, prostate cancer, or any other disease that we can think of? When we can answer this question, make the connection between the disease and the food we eat, because every one of those diseases is a result of the food and drink we put into our bodies.

The food problem is as serious as the disease the food creates. We have been taught to accept disease as a natural part of life and that disease comes with old age, but both premises are not true.

The human body is constantly decaying and renewing itself at the same time. As old cells die new cells take their place. It's the same with the animal body. While alive, animal cells die and new ones take their place.   When an animal dies, there are no new cells being formed. The animal immediately begins to putrefy and rot. When we eat the meat of dead animals, we are eating putrefied and rotten flesh. Cooked food is also dead food. When you cook it, you kill all of the nutrients, vitamins and minerals.

The blood supplies the building material for our body. The blood is made from what we eat and drink. What kind of cells and tissues can be made from blood that is made from dead cooked food and putrefying rotting flesh? This might sound offensively disgusting, but fibroid tumors, prostate cancer, high blood pressure, sugar diabetes, or any of the other diseases that dead food creates are worse than it sounds.

The body is alive. Why would we want to kill ourselves with dead food? That's the same as building a house with rotten timber. If you don't use good wood, the house will fall apart very quickly.

After eating cooked food for all or most of your life, it is not easy to do without. Simply adding more raw fresh organic fruits and vegetables will help anyone who wants to begin to eat a better diet. You can begin the process of improving your health by taking the time to add a little uncooked food to your diet every week until the food is at least 70% to 80% live, uncooked food.

The unhealthy food we eat affects us in the same way that drugs do, wreaking havoc on the health, the thoughts and the emotions of everyone taking drugs. Drugs make it almost impossible to create a healthy, long lasting and loving relationship with a significant other.

Processed food and drugs have had a lot to do with the lack of brotherhood we experience because of the destructive effect bad food and drugs have on the nervous system. The processed food, drugs and chemicals that we put into the body pass through the delicate tissues of the brain and have an adverse effect on the mind. Thus, we are overly sensitive to everything, always ready to defend ourselves or take offense without significant provocation. The single most important asset that we have is the mind. If we take care of the body and the thoughts we choose to think, the machinery that makes us who we are will serve us well.

In December 2007 I went to Honduras to spend time with Dr. Sebi, who I consider the greatest healer in North, South and Central America. One of the many experiences that I enjoyed in this Third World country with this profound healer was riding in his car and going into the indigenous places that seemed like jungles. I remember being fascinated when he would spot a bush or plant, get out of his car, up-root the plant and explain to me how it worked on the body. One time he handed me a twig, told me to break it open so I could inhale the vapors. As I sniffed the twig, I could feel a sensation in my sinuses. Twenty minutes later I was spitting and coughing up mucus and breathing better.

The day after I arrived in Honduras, Dr. Sebi told me that he had been fasting for 30 days and was going to continue to fast for another 60 days. He said that fasting and cleansing the body for 90 days would allow the body to heal itself of any disease. That night I thought about having the privilege to be in the company of this great healer. When I awoke that morning, I informed Dr. Sebi that I intended to join him and fast for as long as I was there (eight days). By the third day I attempted to rise from sitting and became dizzy. Sebi said that was the plaque and toxins loosening up from the brain as a result of the fast and taking his compounds.

Before I went to Honduras I had been eating nothing but uncooked food for two years. One of the things that I learned from Dr. Sebi is cooking natural food does not destroy any of the nutrients because it's natural. Unfortunately, according to Sebi, with the exception of spelt, quinoa, amaranth, teff, kamut and wild rice (grains), portabella and oyster mushrooms, chayote (a vine plant) and dandelion greens, everything else in a grocery store is hybrid or genetically engineered. I also ate a lot of garlic until Sebi explained why garlic is dangerous. Garlic has a ph of 3.9 and anything that is a ph of 2 can kill you. The ph of anything determines if it is alkaline or acid. Anything above 7 is alkaline. Anything below 7 is acid.

Dr. Sebi has earned his acclaimed position as a master healer because he has documented medical proof that he can cure AIDS, cancer, leukemia, sickle cell, sugar diabetes, and many other hard to cure diseases. Go to "you tube" and type his name into your computer and judge for yourself as you listen to the answers he offers those who interview and question him.

Professional athletes who would like to function at the highest level and athletes who are past their prime and would like to prolong their careers – I advise you to research Dr Sebi's.

Dr. Sebi is 76 years young. Fifteen years ago I saw him climb up a 15 foot gym rope in a loft building without using his legs. He stayed to the top of the rope for five minutes talking to those on the ground before he climbed back down, again without using his legs. In 2006 I went to hear Dr. Sebi speak at the Harlem office state building. While he was walking back and forth across the stage speaking to an audience of a few hundred people, I saw him drop to his knees and bounce back up to a standing position all in one motion and continue to talk as if nothing happened, oblivious to the fact that he had blown everyone's mind.

The food we eat has a great deal to do with how

we think, how we feel, and how we act. It is not possible to have a healthy relationship with anyone if we are not eating food that will maintain good health.

The Problem With Women Is Men

Consciousness

Whatever it was, whatever it is, and whatever it may become, doesn't exist without consciousness. Consciousness is the mental faculty that gives us the ability to perceive whatever is going on.

Our consciousness helps to determine every single facet of our existence based on however we choose to think about any and everything.

There is individual consciousness and there is collective consciousness. When we observe someone and come to conclusions concerning what kind of a person we think they might be, the conclusions are based on our own consciousness as well as the other's conscious projection of themselves. When we form opinions about an indigenous group of people in a particular country, we are looking at their collective consciousness from the view of our own collective consciousness. For example, the French have a collective romantic consciousness that they project. The Japanese have a collective business consciousness that they project. Africans have a collective creative consciousness that they project.

Most people know that thoughts are powerful enough to affect the way we feel. This is because thoughts give off a frequency and vibration that can be raised or lowered, depending on what we choose to think about. If we think negative thoughts, we lower the frequency and vibration of our thoughts, which in turn affects our entire body emotionally, physically and spiritually. There are many cases where people lower the frequency and vibration of their thoughts to such an extent that it kills them. This is a result of creating too much stress for the mind or body to deal with.

We can also heal ourselves when the vibrations of the body is raised to a healthy state. We have all had the experience of feeling elated when hearing good news. That is an example of a healthy state. But receiving good news does not keep us in good health. Refusing to pass judgment, living in the moment and learning to love unconditionally raises the frequency and vibration of the mind, body and spirit that maintains good health.

Not very long ago in earth's history, it is said that many people lived for hundreds of years in a healthy mental and physical state. It is definitely possible considering that the glands are designed to maintain the longevity of the body by releasing hormones that could keep the body alive indefinitely. There are studies that show cells can live indefinitely in the right environment.

We don't live as long as we potentially can because it's not a part of our consciousness. Whatever we think is our state (our condition) and how we think of it is what makes it what it is. Our condition is based on our consciousness. We expect to die, and so we die. We focus on our age and make that more important than living our lives, so we age. We look back and we look forward, which maintains the illusion of time instead of the reality of the moment.

The only reality is now, the moment, the present consciousness. When we learn this and how to love unconditionally without passing judgment, our lives can and may go on for as long as we want within the same body. And if it becomes necessary to change bodies in order to continue life, the consciousness can remain without losing its memory.

Have you noticed the difference between the times when you are at one point young and at another point old? It's all in the mind. Your thinking has been cultivated over a period of time based on experience. You don't see things in the same way anymore. You are a different person because you think differently at different points in time. The instant you change your thinking, whatever it is, will no longer be. You changed and it changed. If you wake up tomorrow and you no longer like what was once your favorite food, sport, car, friend, movie, teacher or whatever, it will cease to be. Your new consciousness has created a new reality.

If only five percent of the average person's thoughts are positive, it explains why people subject themselves to the difficulties of life, given that their consciousness is not as proactive as it could be. If people made an effort to think positive and concentrated their levels of consciousness on that form of thinking, the results would be uplifting for everyone.

Although poverty is clearly the economic and political result of compounded oppression, it manifests and thrives because of a collective consciousness that portrays itself as diseased and poverty-stricken. When a group of people is oppressed, the greatest tragedy is that its own self-esteem is taken away. This is true of lower classes, the female gender and various ethnic groups. The group becomes psychologically and physically dependent on others, and is therefore vulnerable to a poverty-stricken consciousness. Thus, the group helps to foster its own diseased and poverty conscious reality.

The rich and poor have collectively created whatever goes on in this country. The poisoned food, the polluted water and air, the mistreatment of each other, the inability to cure current and old diseases, and the disregard we have for elders and children, are problems that we are all responsible for. They would cease to be problems if the collective consciousness chose to obtain solutions and cures.

Whenever a city, state or nation is dissatisfied with its leadership, the people must look to themselves as the solution. Leadership comes from the people who are being led. The collective consciousness of a people is directly responsible for the quality of leadership that is in place.

There are diverse ethnic groups within the U.S. that think differently about the same situations. Within those particular groups, there are people who have different opinions about the same thing. This stops the issues from being resolved, regardless of the amount of time and attention given to those issues. At best, different people may change their minds and positions about something, but the level of confusion remains the same as long as the collective consciousness remains the same. People need to look at the issues that need to be addressed instead of who is being affected by what is happening.

When a group of people, a community, or a state learns to think in the same way regarding a particular situation, the result is powerful, even when the group is incorrect in its thinking (witness Nazi Germany in the 1930's and '40's). As a unified group, the potential to wake up to the correct way can be realized (witness the U.S. Civil Rights Movement of the 1950's and '60's). The people woke up collectively. It's this level of communication and unity that enables a collective consciousness to be powerfully effective.

I used to believe that once we reach a certain spiritual level, we are closer to again becoming one with the Creator. I believed that when this happened, we'd be back where we started and life's journey would be over. I have since changed my view. There is no end to the existence of the inner self.

Within the principle of infinity, there is no beginning and no end. We are and always have been a part of existence. Since everything is and always will be consciousness, our lives go on forever. When a physical body dies, the spirit moves infinitely on to inhabit another body in order to learn. This happens when another woman gives birth to the spirit of another child. We learn lessons along the way or we continue to repeat the same lesson a million lifetimes if necessary until we learn. Anything that creates emotional or physical pain is a lesson that we are still learning.

In The Kybalion, a book containing the seven laws that govern the universe, the very first law is *The Principle of Mentalism*. Everything is mental (consciousness). The entire world and everything in the universe is a mental creation. The second law is *The Principle of Correspondence.* As above, so below; as below, so above. There is always a correspondence between the laws and phenomena of the various planes of being and life. The third law is *The Principle of Vibration.* Everything moves; everything vibrates. Nothing is dead, just degrees of vibration from gross matter to spirit. The fourth law is *The Principle of Polarity.* Everything is dual; everything has poles; everything has its pair of opposites; opposites are identical in nature, but different in degree. The fifth law is *The Principle of Rhythm.* Everything flows, out and in; all things rise and fall; the pendulum-swing manifests in everything. The sixth law is *The Principle of Cause* and *Effect.* Every cause has its effect; every effect has its cause; nothing happens by chance. There are no accidents. The seventh law is *The Principle of Gender.* Everything has its Feminine and Masculine Principle; Gender manifests on all planes.

We all have a responsibility to learn what the natural law and order of things are, so that we can move in harmony with things as they are instead of trying to go against natural law and order. As we move in harmony with things as they are, we move in harmony with ourselves. If we are in harmony with ourselves, everything will be in harmony with us, especially relationships. The Kybalion, written by three initiates, is an excellent book to begin to learn these principles.

The decision to do or not to do anything is only a conscious thought away. Men must use their collective consciousness in a way that will allow them to bond with themselves, and only then are they able to bond with women.

Inside Out or Outside In

The Universe and all of life operates from the inside out. We are blessed with having all of the answers within us to determine what we need for our peace of mind, happiness and spiritual growth. When we relax, think about and feel whatever it is that confronts us, the answer is manifested. When we look within ourselves for answers, we honor the God within us, and the God within us has all the answers.

Many people refer to the alter ego as the ego. The ego is the reflection of our highest consciousness. When we function from the inside-out, we are expressing ourselves through our God consciousness. When we function from the outside-in, we are expressing ourselves through our alter ego, which disconnects us from our God consciousness, giving rise to our disharmonic side. With the outside - in approach, we place obstacles in our way before we get started.

When looking outside of ourselves for acceptance and worth, we lose our self-esteem because it does not allow us to build the faith and trust that we need to have in ourselves. The loss of self-esteem means exactly that we have lost a certain sense of ourselves. The capacity to believe in ourselves and maintain faith and confidence has been compromised. The loss of self-esteem gives birth to fear, guilt and selfishness which does not allow people to be at peace with themselves or each other.

Women are more vulnerable to the outside - in approach because they are more internal and more sensitive than men are. Thus, women are subject to becoming more adversely affected. It's like spilling a small amount of black ink on a pure white blouse. It is very noticeable. Since men are more external, they are not as easily affected by the outside-in approach. When they are so affected, men tend to use their alter egos as an expedient to justify and camouflage this internal weakness. The same amount of black ink on their white shirts will not be as noticeable because the shirt is not as naturally white. Men must cultivate and work on whatever it is. For this reason, whenever and wherever you observe women doing the same negative things that men do, they stand out and are more noticeable.

The loss of self-esteem starts at an early age. When children are able to understand the difference between yes and no, the seeds of low self-esteem can be planted. When a child shows signs of fear or guilt, it indicates low self-esteem. Many parents bully their children, which instills fear. Just as many parents blame their children, which instills guilt. Having patience and letting your children find their own way helps them build confidence through which to address their own challenges.

We also live in a society that places more importance on man made law instead of natural (spiritual) law. Most man made laws are actually rules that restrict and suppress the creative imagination, which leads to more fear and more guilt. Together or separately, fear and guilt lead to low self-esteem because the innate ability to trust yourself is stifled.

When we approach things from outside - in, we satisfy ourselves superficially. We view life from a physical and materialistic perspective. The conversations consist of the amount of money we have, how many women we can get, how many men chase us, the expensive clothes that we have, how comparatively nice the home is, how much the car costs, the dinner parties we go to, and how important we are. Giving these things priority automatically puts us in competition with others, which is why the society is so judgmental.

I have heard women say how tired they are of hearing men brag about themselves. I have heard them laugh among themselves at how often men inflate the stories they tell in order to appear important. One woman mentioned that she would give men like this a number to a pay phone when they ask for her phone number. She said they did not take the time to find out something about her or speak truthfully about themselves without bragging.

I have also heard men talk about how much money women thought should be spent on them, how they would only eat in the most expensive restaurants and stay in the fanciest hotels, or how they would not go out unless they had something new to wear. The polarity that exists between women and men only gets wider with this outside - in approach.

Many men tend to project a selfish consciousness regarding women, and women tend to indiscriminately see men with a negative consciousness. Women set themselves up to be hurt when they indiscriminately think of most men this way, and men help to create fear in women when they are selfish and insensitive. This fear will attract exactly what women are afraid of. The attraction is unavoidable because every thought becomes a reality.

The female friends that women attract will also be those who have similar experiences with men. Thus, the negative consciousness of women regarding men is reinforced. It's like throwing more wood on an already blazing fire.

Just like all women are not the same, all men are not the same. Unless women collectively learn to see men as individuals, they will remain vulnerable to this negative consciousness and continue to repeat their negative experiences over and over again. There are many women who have found lasting love and happiness with men because they did not allow themselves to be part of the collective negative consciousness of other women.

When we approach things from inside - out, we infuse ourselves with positive thinking. We will want to feed our minds with knowledge that leads to a higher consciousness. The inside - out approach is necessary because everyone is different, and being different dictates that you follow yourself not someone else. If we are to understand and appreciate what is happening outside of us, it starts with what is going on inside of us. Whether or not we like or dislike what is happening does not matter. If we accept this approach, it is within our power to deal with all situations and change whatever it is we want to change in life.

Many people believe that it is necessary to understand their mate. It is necessary that we understand ourselves. This can only happen when we approach life from inside - out. We then set ourselves up to get the best out of our relationships because we are in tune with our higher selves and will attract the same type of people.

Pleasure or Pain

As we journey through life, we only have two choices that will help us learn what we are destined to know. Those choices are based on learning through pleasure (making positive choices) or learning through pain (making negative choices). When we learn through positive experiences, the lessons are pleasurable, easy and smooth. When we learn through negative experiences, the lessons are painful, difficult and slow.

Both roads lead to where we need to be. One road has no obstacles that we need to overcome. On this road people are encouraging us and offering their help unconditionally. We now have time to enjoy the walk and to appreciate what we learn while on the journey. This is the road of positive experiences.

The other road involves people dictating to us how we should live our lives; or they are trying to manipulate us for their own benefit. As we continue on this road, there are also those who offer to assist us while putting conditions on the help. Once we get past the manipulators and ignore the conditions, someone else builds a barrier to try and block the progress. This is the road of negative experiences.

Based on the experiences that most of us have had and the ability to understand how things are, I think we all can agree that the society we live in is saddled with a lot of baggage. This baggage has produced many dysfunctional families and has conditioned many of us to accept learning the lessons of life through pain.

When it comes to relationships, the type of guidance we receive from the parents and the type of environment we are raised in have a big influence in the type of person we choose as a mate. If you are scolded, yelled at, abused or beaten as a child, the foundation is being laid to learn through negative experiences. If you are spoiled and given everything you want as a child, the foundation is also being laid to learn through negative experiences.

When you start school, your familiarity with pain becomes a part of your interaction with students who have had very similar occurrences in life (like attracts like). The negative experiences are now being reinforced by others negative experiences. Thus, students fight, rob each other, beat up teachers, play hooky, sell drugs, and engage in other activities that result in pain. By the time you are ready for a serious relationship, your experiences have not prepared you to have a fulfilling and loving one.

Learning to walk the road of positive experiences starts in the home. There are parents who understand that guiding and teaching children without trying to control them is the best approach they can take to prepare children to grow with positive frames of mind. This understanding helps to instill a sense of confidence and freedom of thought that children need. Children who have been raised this way have wonderful imaginations and a profound sense of self that will not be subjugated by a society of rules and regulations that restrict and suppress the creative imagination.

If we took the time to weigh the positive against the negative choices, most of us would much rather learn through positive experiences. That's what makes life interesting and exciting. We do have a choice and the opportunity to think about what we do. It's just a matter of being aware of what we want and giving thought to our choices.

To learn through positive experiences is to walk the road that has no obstacles or to turn stumbling blocks into stepping-stones. As a friend of mine says on his answering machine to aid the listener in walking this positive road, "If you want to have peace and happiness in your life, do only those things that bring you joy." Of course, this is not as easy as it sounds. Many of us have not been taught to understand what joy really means. Joy means anything that gives us pleasure. However, the greatest joy is sharing with others. When we share with others, we are really sharing with ourselves because everybody we come in contact with represents that part of us that is in them. When we accept this truth, our joy becomes constant.

Before we make a choice, we should think about the result to be derived from the experience. Many things that appear pleasurable actually give us pain. For example, there are many people who believe that they actually obtain pleasure from taking drugs. Yet, once the drugged state of mind wears off, pain usually ensues. The money spent, the time wasted, the damage done to one's mental and physical health, and the misery that it might have caused others, are all painful experiences. If the end result is painful, the pleasurable beginning was only an illusion to help teach us what we needed to know. If we get caught up in the illusion, many of us find ourselves moving in the dark for years with no desire to step into the light.

We cannot move into the light if we accept the illusion as reality. We will remain in the dark without really knowing it or remain in the dark until the pain motivates us to walk into the light. It's just like someone who smokes telling you that they understand the damage that they are doing to themselves by smoking. If they really understood, they would be able to stop. Why walk around in the dark when you can turn on the switch to light the room? When we light up the room, we can see and understand things for what they are, instead of what we guessed or what someone told us.

There are many illusions that we accept in everyday life. "Save the children" sounds good, but we need to "save the adults." Then, children will automatically be saved because adults raise children. "Where there's a will there's a way" also sounds good, but "where there's love is the way." If my will is opposed to your will, there will be conflict. These misguided thoughts and others like them prepare us to accept illusion over reality. Many people simply accept darkness over the light because they don't think. They allow themselves to accept other people's ill-advised perception which is not consistent with learning.

How do we get off the road that teaches us through negative experiences? We have to begin to look at life in a different way. Having an open mind is the key to doing this. An open mind will help us turn negative experiences into positive ones. Every lemon can be turned into lemonade. This can be done when we accept an experience without judgment and realize that the given experience is a message to help us.

Yes, it does take time to form new ways of doing things, especially when most people have embraced and accepted negative programming as a result of living in a judgmental society. But being aware that a different approach is needed is the first step in making a difference. Some of us can change overnight.

It's all a mindset. When you can reset the thinking, the thoughts create the change and become a reality.

Many of us withdraw as a result of becoming self-conscious. We are filled with fear because we believe the negative experiences (all illusions) are huge. In these situations we are passing judgement on whatever is happening. We must accept the experience for what it is and move forward without weighing ourselves down with pain that comes from judgment. We should remind ourselves that the same degree that the pendulum swings negatively is the same degree that the pendulum will swing positively. The pendulum will always swing back. Thus, if you are doing something that gives you great pain, you can do something that gives you great pleasure.

What if every time you get into a disagreement with a mate, nothing is resolved? Not only does no one win the argument, but sometimes we lose a significant other for reasons that did not amount to very much.

The majority of conflicts occur because one partner is not allowing the other to evolve and learn without interfering. We seem to become insecure when our significant other doesn't respond to situations in the same way that we do. We often spend a lot of time interfering with a significant other's movie while needing a director and producer for our own movie. Life is a journey with obstacles in our path put there by us to help us learn. If we can accept and appreciate this, it will be easier to handle the challenges that confront us.

What would you be losing if the next time an argument began you stopped and said, "You might be right; let me think about it?" You would lose nothing. You'd be preventing an argument, and helping to maintain the pleasure to be reaped in the relationship. This non-threatening approach can be applied to many of our potentially disruptive situations.

Living in the Moment

Instead of focusing on the moment, we seem to be programmed to look backward into the past and forward into the future. When in truth, the past and the future are just illusions that we create. The only reality we can verify is right now, this moment. Relationships should also be grounded in the moment and not in the past or the future.

When we collapse the illusion of time, the past, present and future happen simultaneously. At this very moment we are all we have ever been and all we ever will be. Whatever thoughts we now have come from past experiences and determine our future experiences. This is why it is so important to carefully choose what we want to think about, both in terms of content and quality. With every thought, we are creating the next experience. It doesn't matter who or what the thought is about, it is set in motion to happen.

All of the great thinkers throughout history have had conflicting views about many things. However, they have all collectively agreed on one important truth and that is everything is mental and thoughts are things that manifest into physical reality. This is what makes life so wonderful. We have the free will to think any thought we choose in order to create any reality that we want at the moment we think the thought. Yet most of us don't really believe that thoughts are things and that the invisible is more powerful than the visible. Doesn't everything start with a thought? Isn't it true that thoughts cannot be seen? Maybe this is why the phrase "patience is a virtue" has been passed on from generation to generation. Someone obviously understood that people needed to be reminded of this important aspect of humanity: be patient until the thoughts manifest. Understand that the manifestations may not appear the way we imagined them. For this to happen, the thoughts should be well grounded and unencumbered by human vices in order to bear ripe fruit.

Life is a journey and one of the greatest lessons we can learn is that people are like water seeking their own level. It's a personal journey in a collective environment. We are all doing exactly what the individual level of consciousness needs to do at that moment in order to learn exactly what's needed.

It seems that we live in a world where people would rather learn from unnecessary pain instead of joy. When we don't accept joy as the teacher, we make it possible for severe pain to show us the next lesson. If there is someone we look upon as lowly or someone we know who is caught up in serious trauma or drama, what we are witnessing is someone learning from the pain they have chosen to learn from. Many of us have not realized or understood that pain is a great teacher, and we all choose the particular level of pain for the lesson that we need. Sometimes, according to the level of consciousness, the pain is so great and the drama so intense that we cannot believe that we are responsible for this particular experience. This is especially true when we associate how unhappy we are with what we are going through at the moment. However, this is exactly what we have chosen for ourselves in order to learn.

How you (looking from the outside) feel about what anyone else is or is not doing is not relevant to anyone or anything. While you can empathize and sympathize, you can't truly feel for another person, nor can you truly know how another person feels. When it is time, each one of us will get off any one road and on to the next. While it is true that you can help someone else deal with an experience, you can't really save anyone else. What you can do is "assist," which is different from "insist." You must take care to distinguish between "assist" and "insist," for the more you insist that others change their lives simply because of your opinion of what's good for them, the more your insistence will be resisted. Keep in mind that what you often insist upon has a way of running parallel to the work you need to do with regards to the particular journey you are on. Many relationships would survive if we allowed others to learn their particular lesson without our "insistent" interference.

In today's hi-tech society, most people keep journals and diaries as aids to help them in their life's progress. Indigenous people understood that keeping faith in the spirit that dwells within them helps to create whatever they desire and require. They knew that thoughts are made to manifest as things. They knew that the mind is like the ground on a farmer's land; whatever kind of seed is planted becomes the type of plant that will grow.

Earl Nightingale, a motivational speaker since the 1950s, makes a wonderful comparison between the land and the human mind. He offers the following analogy: Suppose a farmer has some fertile land in which to grow crops. The land gives the farmer a choice. He can plant whatever he chooses; the land doesn't care. The farmer has two seeds. One seed is corn and the other seed is nightshade, a deadly poison. The farmer digs two holes and plants both seeds. He covers up the two holes and waters and cultivates both plants. So, what happens? Invariably the land returns whatever is planted.

He says, the land doesn't care about what is planted. It returns the poison nightshade in the same wonderful abundance that it returns the corn.

The human mind is far more fertile and far more incredible than the land, but it works in the same way. It doesn't care what we plant in our minds. Love, courage, patience and faith are plants that must be returned to us if those are the seeds that we plant. If we plant success, we will succeed. If we plant failure, we will fail. Hate confusion, anxiety and fear, are also plants that must be returned to us if those are the seeds that we plant. They lead to misunderstanding and a lack of communication in relationships.

We live in a society that has placed more importance on the calculating intellect than it has on the intuitive mind. Thus we focus on explaining everything. And if things don't work out, we explain some more. While all things need to be understood, nothing really needs to be explained, or justified. When we pay too much attention to justifying ourselves, we become caught up in the opinions (prejudices) of others. This is more in line with passing judgment than in understanding the nature of things.

The technological society motivates most of us to cultivate and develop the intellect through modern technology. There are computers in all of the modern technological gadgets we now use to make life better. They can find solutions and answers to just about everything. However, it is necessary that we create a balance between our intellectual side and our intuitive side. It is also necessary to keep in mind that the advanced technology can take us outside of ourselves to the point that we are neglecting, and in some cases, forgetting to look inside ourselves for answers and solutions. Remember that computers are designed by peoples' consciousness. Is some of their morality injected into the programs?

A friend once mentioned that he teaches children to do their math problems in their heads instead of using a calculator. He said he was concerned about them using the calculator and not developing skills. He also had reservations about computers for the same reason. While computers are a wonderful source of information, we must realize that we can rely too much on computers and end up stifling the creative and intuitive gifts we have.

This is another important reason why we should allow the children to grow without constraints. Children are very intuitive. The choices they make are usually correct. Unless we see them walking into harm's way, it's best to allow them to walk their journey without adults trying to control the process or the outcome. In this way, their intuitive gift gets stronger with every experience. This builds self-confidence, faith, and trust, which ultimately evolve into realizing higher degrees of peace, love and happiness.

We all know people who did not finish high school and therefore had limited instructive skills, yet some how became very successful. They intuitively understood that the accomplishments would be determined by the faith in themselves. They were determined to remain focused in order to succeed and the success could not be denied.

While developing the intuitive side is vital, by itself, it is not enough. While learning from the past helps us develop, by itself, it is not enough. It is necessary that we use both sides of the scale, the intuitive and the intellect. In this way we may guide ourselves to the best of our ability on whatever journey we choose to take.

Reading is a modern form of story telling. Indigenous people used the spoken word to tell stories.

The modern society dictates that books take the place of the spoken word in order for us to teach and discover the lessons that the ancestors learned and wanted to pass on to us.

Nothing in the world is new, everything is in a cycle. When we accept and understand this truth, we will also know that we have been here before and will return again to repeat the same experiences until we learn what we need to know in order to move forward. Thus, natural law and metaphysical understanding are tools that we need to help guide us on the journey. Since story telling is a thing of the past, books help us in the research. When we read, we are learning from the experiences of others that are sharing the information and knowledge.

With regards to both reading and story telling, they can only add to, not substitute for personal experiences. Learning through our own actions is what the journey is all about. There are no mistakes on anyone's journey. Every experience is needed. Our willingness to learn through our actions and to accept our results as lessons helps to develop the intuitive side of our nature, as well as our intellectual side. We all would like to be successful in our relationships. If our thoughts are in the past or the future, how can we succeed in the present with our significant other?

Think about your relationship in a relaxed and loving way. If you see yourself in a successful and happy relationship, you will achieve it. If you have doubts, your reason for doubting becomes your reality. In a three-dimensional world whatever you perceive will be, just as planting a seed in the ground will grow a plant.

Unconditional Love

Expressing unconditional love makes us the wonderful spiritual beings we truly are. It starts with "self first." Unconditional love for yourself is the foundation for everything positive that happens in your life. It's like being fearless. When you are fearless, you allow yourself to rise above the drama and learn whatever your lessons are. There is no blame, fight or resisting yourself. Thus, you are able to unconditionally love yourself, which creates a higher frequency and vibration. You will not have to continue to repeat the same painful lessons over and over again. When you live fearlessly, the lesson has been learned (all of life is a learning experience) and you can move on to your next lesson within the lightness of your being instead of the heaviness of the drama. You have raised your consciousness and exhibit natural instincts.

When you are on this path, you can truly love yourself, your mate and other people. Your love for others and especially your mate will not be based on conditions, such as, "If you love me, I will love you; if you do this for me, I will do that for you; if you stop doing this, I'll stop doing that." These are conditions that you have placed on yourself while believing that you have placed them on others. Whatever you try to do to someone else, you are doing to yourself.

When love is based on conditions, what you do or feel will be based on what someone else does or feels. It's the same as letting someone else's opinion become your reality. You will also try to let your opinion become their reality. When people think this way, the seeds of unconditional love have not been planted because you are thinking (outside of yourself) through someone else. This approach doesn't work because there are no two people alike and no one can feel or think like you.

When you base your love on conditions, you create a situation that will change when the conditions change. This kind of love is used as a basis for friendship, marriage and raising children. Is it any wonder that we live in a society where friendship, marriage and raising children are full of serious challenges? Love based on conditions, is not love.

Ever since I can remember, the expression *"fight fire with fire"* has been a popular saying. Do you know what happens when you fight fire with fire? You get twice as much fire back and you get burned twice as many times. We need to fight fire with water in order to put the fire out. This is why unconditional love is the answer. It's like water, putting out a fire.

We feed two birds with one seed when we practice unconditional love. We live through our karma without resistance and put ourselves on a path that helps us to learn through joy by making choices with consciousness instead of making selfish choices. We all have karma. Anything in life that we resist, fight or blame on others is an experience that must be repeated.

Every thought and feeling carries a frequency and vibration associated with our level of consciousness. Unconditional love is the highest vibrational feeling we can have. This is why it is important for us to cultivate unconditional love. We then won't judge people or get feelings they have

167

wronged us when things don't work out the way we would like them to. When we have knowledge of judgment and karma, we know that it is our karma manifesting and ourselves that we judge.

Our mates are the closest people to us and we are constantly learning from them and them from us. We cannot take it personally when the messenger delivers our karmic lesson to us. If the lesson is based on pain and we personalize it, we will want to get even with the messenger by striking back. We will think thoughts of hate and revenge, which lowers our frequency level and keeps us repeating the same painful lesson until we get it right.

If the lesson is joyful and we personalize it, we will want to reward the messenger. If we reward the messenger, the principle of polarity allows us to understand that when the pendulum swings back the other way and the lesson is painful we will want to harm the messenger. Our sincere gratitude and unconditional love for whom it is felt is reward enough.

If we are being mistreated, it is difficult to turn the other cheek. These situations dictate that we should respond in the same way. Sometimes our mates and other people know how to push all the right buttons in order to irritate and annoy us. When we can find the courage to stay composed, it helps to strengthen our character and keeps us on the path to a greater understanding.

Just as unconditional love is the highest thought frequency we can have, hate is the lowest thought frequency we can have. The frequency of hate is just as powerful as the frequency of love. If we hold on to that frequency long enough, it can destroy our inner strength.

Unconditional love creates the joy that allows us to think and vibrate with the lightness of being. Such a frequency keeps us on the path of a higher consciousness and will help us stabilize our relationships.

The same unconditional love that one feels for a newborn baby is the same unconditional love we must cultivate for ourselves. Everything starts from within and moves outward. Understanding this relation between the inner and outer side allows us to unconditionally love as we began with ourselves.

If everyone were to cultivate and nurture the thought of unconditional love, imagine the level of consciousness that would vibrate throughout the planet. The world would be continuously reinforcing itself, raising levels of energy with positive results. There would be no wars, starvation, crime or disease. The world would be a place of prosperity based on cooperation and joy instead of competition and pain.

Judgment

We live in a judgmental society that judges people based on what they think people should or should not be doing. Every time we pass judgment on someone or something we are seeing things about ourselves that we have not accepted. We cannot feel what anyone else feels nor understand what anyone else understands. We are all at different stages of learning exactly what we need to know. So why are we judging others for the same lessons that we all are destined to learn?

We are the orchestrators of our fate. We are the producers, directors and actors in the movie of life. The movie represents things about our life that we see when we look outside of ourselves into our world. We can only experience that which is inside us. This is the key to understanding everything that happens to us.

Most of us are familiar with sayings such as, "Birds of a feather flock together," and, "like attracts like." Well, those sayings are based on very real scientific phenomena.

People who go to health conventions and health expositions are aware that their auras can be captured with special photographic equipment that can tell what kind of energy is coming from their bodies, based on their thoughts.

Thoughts give off a frequency and a vibration that attract people whose thoughts are on the same frequency and vibration as our own. Thus, the "birds of a feather..."

In other words, one is attracting oneself. And so it is that judging others is exactly the same as judging oneself. For when we sit in judgment of other people, we are really facing a mirror reflection of who we are. This mirror image of ourselves helps us to learn by observing what we see going on before us.

Preston Johnson, an enlightened teacher, says on his C D, "If judges in court knew that they would also be judged as many times that they passed judgment on others, they would seek another profession. Imagine having to come back in future lives to become every one of the people that you had sentenced to a jail term and in some cases sentenced to death."

Judging people on the basis of what you don't like is the same as judging them on the basis of what you do like. The Principle of Polarity, one of the seven laws that govern the universe, is why there's no difference between both extremes. Everything has its opposite, and opposites are different degrees of the same thing. For example, if you look at a thermometer, where does hot begin and cold end? If you also observe someone who always praises people for being clean and can't stand to see people who are less clean, this person is actually looking at a reflection of self. That we engage in the act of judging lets us know that whatever we are passing judgment on is a sore point that is still inside of us. If it were not, there would be no inclination to judge. We would accept it for what it is.

In general, neither women nor men are taught spiritual law. We often react to each other without having true knowledge of the price we pay in pain and suffering when our reaction is judgmental.

Many people believe that the Creator is in heaven passing judgment on humanity. The Creator is loving Cosmic Energy and does not pass judgment on anyone or anything. Humans are the ones who judge themselves and other humans. If the Creator were passing judgment, mankind would be a pawn to play with and free will would be non-existent.

We are part of infinity and with infinity all things are possible. People don't see themselves as God-like because they are too busy judging themselves on the basis of being or not being sinful. But there is no sin; there are only lessons to be learned. Passing judgment about anyone or anything stops us from learning lessons and accepting ourselves. If we cannot accept ourselves as we are, we cannot love ourselves as we are. This kind of thinking sets us up to pass judgment on ourselves.

"If only I had that, I could do this!"

"If you had not said what you said, this would not have happened."

"The minute you did that, you stopped me from getting this."

The above statements are examples of comments that act to slow down the learning process. These statements are based on a lack of understanding that we are responsible for any and everything that we do or do not do. The people in your life are exact reflections of you. You always attract your own reflection. Everyone in your life represents some part of you, as you reflect some part of them in their life. One Creator, one Consciousness and one Universe mean that we are not separate but connected, and part of every one that we see in front of us. If you look closely at the people you have established any kind of relationship with, you will recognize traits about yourself in them.

Every woman that a man knows reflects some part of her own female element that is within him. He sees himself when he sees her. He is looking at another part of his own reflection. This is true of women as well. Every man that a woman knows reflects some part of her own male element that she recognizes in him. She is likewise looking at the male part of herself. Therefore, a mate reflects that much more of you (and vice versa) than other potential mates. It should follow that if what is being reflected causes either person pain or joy, the pain or joy is affecting the other person as well. It just becomes a matter of time before one's karma creates the joy or pain for the other person. Whatever it is, it is. If you don't judge it, you won't become the judgment or be judged by it.

Whenever we pass judgment on anything we multiply it. Addressing anger with anger is an anger judgment; we will get more anger back. Addressing violence with violence is a violent judgment; we will get more violence back. We all know people who express themselves in this way ("An eye for an eye"). These modes of thinking give rise to the events that wind up on the front page of the daily newspapers. These modes of thinking have laid the groundwork for all of the misery we subject ourselves to.

When I was growing in to manhood, I had a lot of pent-up anger. In order to release this anger, I found myself fighting all the time for reasons that made no sense. I wound up joining the Golden Gloves to obtain a release for the anger. For six or seven years I would go to the gym to box and train believing that I was helping to solve the anger issues. It helped to keep me in good health but it did very little for the anger. I stayed angry and challenged everybody and everything. Anger is a mindset based on how we perceive things. Most people are filled with anger and frustration because they have not tried to cultivate their spiritual side or learn natural law.

Every culture has adopted man-made laws that people follow that make it possible to maintain order. These man made laws have the morality of the consciousness of the lawmakers. There are also natural laws and a natural order to the Universe that we should also be aware of. These laws always affect our lives. More often than not, too many countries and too many people try to go against and break the natural law and order of things. However, we cannot break or conquer natural law without going against and destroying ourselves. In order to achieve the satisfaction that we seek in life, we must turn our attention inward and look outside of ourselves less.

When we learn not to pass judgment and accept that we are responsible for everything that happens to us, it will help us achieve the best that life has to offer.

Karma

We come into this world with a soul that carries the sum total of past lives. This sum total represents the knowledge and information from past lives that predetermine what happens to us in this present life. We call this sum total of life karma. When parents understand and accept this principle, they will allow children to realize their destiny by letting them develop and grow without constraints.

There is a lot written about "predestination" versus "free will." They both work together to affect the outcome of what happens to us. What we did in past lives determines the conditions in the present one. However, through free will, we have the opportunity to change what happens to us in the future by raising our consciousness.

When we judge the past, we must repeat that past experience because we have made it a part of our consciousness. This keeps us from living in the moment. We go around in circles and find ourselves in a pattern that we can't seem to escape (much like *Ground Hog Day*, starring Bill Murray). When we are preoccupied with the future, it creates the same problem; we lose sight of the present. The only way to have control over the future is to take conscious control of what we do in the moment. We create and predetermine our karmic future the moment we make a choice about whatever is happening now.

The past, the present and the future are one and the same. While they are on different frequencies, they exist at the same time. With Infinity there is no time or space. Just as the Creator is beyond time and space, we are also beyond time and space. Our lives infinite parts of the whole, guiding us to a higher consciousness.

At this moment we are all we ever were and all we ever will be. All of the lives that we have ever lived and ever will live exist within us right now. Even though past lives have predetermined our present state, we can have an effect on our future through the conscious choices we make at the moment we choose. Most of our choices are based on pleasure or pain. There is no good, no bad, no right or wrong choice. It's all a learning experience.

Whoever we are sharing life with is there for a reason. Once the novelty of the relationship wears off, the reason begins to be clear. What if we find ourselves constantly dealing with issues that we can't seem to resolve? Suppose every time we look up there are more challenges for us with no end in sight. This is simply karma manifesting itself. When this is understood and accepted, we will be able to learn and move forward. If it is not understood, we will stay stuck, repeating the same old lesson until we get tired of the physical, mental and emotional stress and think about things differently.

If there is something happening in a relationship that we don't like, free will allows us to address it to improve the situation. When we address it with unconditional love, our consciousness is raised and we can move forward. When we judge, or blame, we move very slowly and must repeat the same painful lesson for as many times as we look outside of ourselves to come up with answers. When people think with a sense of blame, they usually separate and bring the same challenge to their next relationship.

When we place blame and pass judgment, we attract people with the same thought vibration that we have. In order to break the cycle that has each of us passing the baton of blame back and forth, we must accept total responsibility for what is happening. This is the only way to find answers to the challenges we face.

We are all learning lessons so that we can get to the next level of our evolution. Karma is the teacher that determines how fast we move on the journey. Whether or not we learn through pain or learn through pleasure is determined by our karma. If we committed painful acts upon others in past experiences, our karmic debt will repeat the same kind of experiences for us. There is no way to avoid it. However, when we live consciously in the moment, embrace unconditional love, and refrain from passing judgment, we erase the karmic debt.

Suppose you and a mate choose to move into new relationships because you recognize that the one you are in is not where you were meant to stay. The two of you were there to learn from each other. In order to get the best from the experience you can think of yourselves as two people who were brought together to help each other on the journey. Consequently, you should be conscious not to abuse or mistreat anyone because everyone around you is there to help you learn something about yourself.

Out of love, the ancestors left us; live in the moment, unconditional love and no judgment in order to give us tools to solve the challenges of life. We just happen to be a society that takes this knowledge for granted, so we suffer.

The Problem With Women Is Men

Polygamy or Monogamy

There are several terms that we can be clear about before we read this chapter. Polygamy is the general term for "one mate, many mates"; polygyny is the specific term for "one male, several females"; and polyandry is the specific term for "one female, several males." In this chapter I use the generally accepted term polygamy to explain my views and why.

Polygamy or Monogamy, which way works best?

There are many people and many cultures that believe the practice of polygamy is the way that marriage is naturally meant to be. There are also many reasons to support their beliefs.

Women give birth to more girl than boy babies. This implies that a monogamous relationship, one man for one woman, is not the natural order of nature. If there are not enough men to go around, women have to compete for the affections of men. If every man were paired with one woman, there would be a lot of lonely women who would not have a man as a mate. Do you think the Creator meant for women to be lonely? It's become increasingly clear that monogamy creates loneliness and leads to competition among women. This competition between women has created jealousy, deception and lying amongst them. Thus, the natural bonding that women would enjoy does not exist. The fact that polygamy is and was successfully practiced in many countries helps to support this belief. It is also believed that polygamous relationships among certain animals are a sign from the Creator for people to emulate.

Most people living in America accept and practice monogamy, so we are familiar with the pros and cons revolving around a monogamous relationship. Yet we have accepted the negative attributes of monogamy without addressing them. In spite of the fact that in a monogamist system men are supposed to have only one wife, promiscuity, adultery, prostitution and other factors we live with ensure a situation where many men have more than one sexual partner. This automatically means that women will also have more than one sexual partner, as each leaves the other in search of another. This is not the foundation upon which to build a healthy relationship.

Love and trust in a significant other is a must in order for both partners to experience the bliss of a monogamous marriage. These essential factors can create the joy of living between two people that can help them overcome adversity. This harmony allows communication to flow as easily as breathing. The fear and concern regarding acceptance of one's feelings and innermost thoughts is non-existent. The simple pleasures in life are more enjoyable and both partners acquire a peace and serenity that affects friends and family, especially their children, in a positive way. This bliss adds years to a couple's life as a result of their having less stress. However, very few couples achieve this monogamous bliss because possessiveness and selfishness are byproducts of monogamy. How often have you heard the phrases "my man," or "my woman?" These are statements that imply ownership. Anything you own, you also want to control. Any attempt to control someone else's life naturally leads to pain and suffering. The unhappy marriages and high divorce rate attest to this fact.

Without trust and unconditional love, marriage becomes a game of musical chairs, spreading diseases and personal misery. This form of irresponsible interaction has created lasting polarity between the sexes. Barriers are created instead of being broken down.

According to Dr. William Richardson, "There are women who would rather tolerate a cheating husband than be in polygamy. Because most adulterous relationships are secretive, they figure what they don't know in its entirety, won't hurt them. But nothing could be further from the truth. Ignorance is not bliss. Cheating and deception in marriage can open the door to low self-esteem, extreme jealousy, hatred, violence, addictions, suicide, venereal disease, aids and other horrors from hell."

Polygamy as an alternative lifestyle is another matter that we do not fully understand. Most people in America have been socialized to oppose polygamous relationships. Since it is obvious that most men have problems maintaining a monogamous relationship, women's opposition to polygamy is quite understandable. At present, too many men are not showing enough respect to the one woman they have a relationship with. The numbers of women who are frustrated and disappointed in a mate support this fact.

There are not enough men to go around and the ones that are here don't seem to use their understanding of the situation in the best interests of both parties. Until men address these issues, everybody loses out. Are there well-informed men around? Of course there are! And knowledgeable men must take intelligent steps in order to find solutions that will maintain stable relationships.

Women are biologically stronger than men are. Women live longer than men and a larger percentage of females live to be 100 years of age. There are also fewer miscarriages and stillbirths of female fetuses than male fetuses. The sperm cells that create girl babies are slower but swim longer than the ones that create male babies. The sperm cells that create boy babies are faster, but they die more quickly. Thus, more female sperm cells reach the ova first. Most species on earth produce more females than males as nature's way of securing their survival. These are reasons to justify a polygamous form of marriage.

The Bible says "be fruitful and multiply." I think this is one of the most important arguments that support polygamy as a way of life. Men can have hundreds of babies while women can only have a few.

Today, women are more career-focused than ever before. Their professional interest requires babysitters, housekeepers, and day care centers. The alternative is not having any children at all. Over the years, babysitters and day care centers have proven to be risky solutions and settings regarding the degree of safety and well being of the children involved. Trading motherhood for a career seems like a heavy price to pay. When women choose careers over bearing and raising children, they lose many of their feminine attributes because they try to compete with men. Women have found it very difficult to compete with men without acting in the same aggressive way that men act.

As most women can testify, housekeeping is a full time job. How can anyone maintain a career and effectively raise and maintain a family? When more than one woman is in a household helping to carry out responsibilities, the challenges that arise are easier to deal with.

In polygamous relationships, the sister-wives alleviate the hardships that result from women having outside careers when the man is off dealing with his career. In other cultures where polygamy used to be a way of life, the natural circumstances of living in the same township and knowing your neighbors made polygamy easier to appreciate and accept. High levels of co-operation and harmony existed because the whole community acted as one. The community helped to instill and maintain levels of responsibility that men lived up to in order for women not to feel jealous or threatened by their sister-wives.

In addition to more females being born than males, there are a lot of men in the prison system. The United States has a higher number of men locked up in prison than any other country. At the beginning of 1970, there were 250,000 men in our prison system. Ten years later, there were 500,000 men in prison. By 1990, there were well over 1,000,000 men in prison.

Today there are more than 2,000,000 men incarcerated.[5] As a side effect, over one million youth belong to street gangs, and hundreds of thousands are confused, lost, orphaned, abandoned, drug addicted, homicidal and suicidal.

The stress and added responsibility placed upon women who have mates in prison and children out of control and dying in the streets are enormous. Women find that they have to be mother, father and breadwinner to children while also serving as the base through which they somehow maintain a household.

If polygamy were an alternative, male responsibility would be the key that would determine the success or failure of this form of marriage and divorce would be non-existent.

I have looked at the statistics in many countries regarding women to men ratio and the average is something like 1.6 men to 1 women. I dispute these statistics because the survival of a species requires more females than males being born. It seems to me that these questionable statistics are purposely reported

---

[5] About.com: US Government Info, U.S. Prison Population Tops 2 Million

because it helps maintain a monogamous society. However, if the statistics are somehow accurate, nature compensated because men go to war, lock themselves up in prison, and women live longer.

The Problem With Women Is Men

Human Becoming

We are not really human beings; we are human becomings because we are constantly evolving and becoming something more with each new experience.

Some of us evolve quickly and some of us evolve as if we are not learning at all. Some of us think and grow within a large area of consciousness, while others think and grow within a smaller area of the consciousness. The key to being able to evolve and appreciate the experience as a human, who is becoming, is to have an open mind.

With an open mind, we can't seem to learn and gather information fast enough. We appreciate being the student and the teacher at the same time. The open mind helps us to receive and share knowledge from a limitless number of sources. We are not concerned about who we might be receiving the information from, who we might be sharing the information with, or who is learning more than we are. Those are mental traps that slow us down.

If the mind is closed, little will come in and little will go out. If the mind is closed, whatever information we think we are receiving is turned into something we want it to be instead of what it is (a collection of knowledge from a collective consciousness).

We all know people who only accept information to suit their purposes. It's the same way when they want to let information out. The little "brain doctors" of the mind have already "operated" and turned the information into what they would like it to be. Thus, they give people an opinion instead of passing on factual data. With a closed mind, we learn and evolve slowly.

Sometimes we run into people we haven't seen in a long time and discover that they have changed for the worse. It might be a professional person who has given up on life and is now a derelict. It might be a once happy person who is now bitter about life. They are still learning through pain so their evolution is slow.

The open mind allows us to accept and appreciate the growth of others as well as ourselves, whether the growth is through pleasure or pain (positive or negative experiences).

As we accept people whom we intend to create significant relationships with, being aware of their growth as well as our own is important. When people can do this with an open mind, they are better able to grow together and experience the journey in harmony. Is there anything better than growing and evolving with someone you are in love with?

Many couples separate because one partner outgrows the other. That one person outgrows another is an indication that they are not meant to stay together. They get together to learn from each other and then move on. The relationship takes place to fine-tune them for another relationship. If people are not abusing each other, this is a good thing.

I have observed in the media and through my own observations the drama that takes place when one partner tries to keep the other from severing the relationship. There's nothing wrong with moving on if things are not working out. You either learned what you needed to know or you could not learn from that experience and it's still time to move on. Remember, if you did not learn from that experience, you are destined to repeat it. You might mention to a mate that the two of you were brought together to learn what you both needed to know but were not meant to stay together.

If people are mistreating each other, that's also part of the learning experience that is needed. If we can accept this understanding and offer information without judgment, it will help us learn faster. If we can not do this, we will suffer until we can. Conflict indicates resistance to growth and slows down the progress of anything you attempt to do. If the mind is open, we will respect each other's right to learn so that everyone can move to the next lesson in life.

We do not live in a society where learning is a priority. As a result of this, we evolve very slowly through pain because we lack the knowledge that would aid us on the journey.

What is life but a journey of experiences that allows us to learn and move to the next level of that same journey? Why do we live in a society where learning has to be connected to pain?

Education is supposed to be the process through which we obtain the information that we need so that the journey can be a pleasurable one. I am not just referring to academic education, since half of that is really training. I mean education that teaches us all of the essentials of life as it relates to our physical, mental, spiritual and emotional capacities.

From infancy, children should be taught the information that will help them to grow into well-rounded adults. The information and knowledge they can acquire would help them to enjoy and appreciate the constant evolution of themselves. Can you imagine what adults would be like if, as children, they learned unconditional love, living in the moment and no judgment?

If children were made aware of the growth and evolution of their minds, bodies, emotions and spirit, they would not attach themselves to things as adults do. They would understand how to accept the experience for what it is, learning. Children would be excited and look forward to learning about themselves. However, adults have not been taught what they should know and that does not allow them to teach children properly. A whole new generation would have a refreshing sense of self if adults introduced a new approach to education and learning in order to properly teach the next generation.

The lack of knowledge and information and the labor-oriented education we do get has slowed humanity down to a crawl. In spite of the fact that we now live in the 21st century, mentally we are still on horseback. However, learning how to look at things objectively is necessary to evolve and become the best that we can be.

Friendship

Friendship, like love, does not automatically work because we want it to work. People who are lovable are able to receive love. People who are friendly are able to make friends. Like love, friendship is cultivated over a period of time and is based on integrity and sincerity.

Today friendship appears to be based on need and desire. As in love, this form of friendship has a lot of unspoken conditions attached to it that are related to how much money one has, the amount of material wealth one possesses, or what one can do for someone else. In time, true friendship could become a thing of the past.

Wealthy and famous people often get a rude awakening when they lose their fame and fortune, and in the process lose half the number of people who are supposed to be their friends. The rest of us experience similar reactions from those we think are our friends when we stop providing whatever it is they need.

This is not too difficult to understand when we observe that all of the major cities are overcrowded with people trying to reach the same goals. In addition to the competition, we live on top of each other like sardines in a can and pay too much attention to securing some level of wealth while disregarding the rights of others. Under these conditions, it's easy to understand why we compare ourselves to crabs in a barrel.

It is virtually impossible for people with a crab-barrel mentality to cultivate true friendship. When the friendship is tested or challenged, they fail to measure up. Most people are not willing to let friendship outweigh what they think they need.

Many new ideas tend to go against the grain of old ideas. Unconditional friendship is a new idea that most of us are unwilling to accept. We give lip service to friendship in the same way that we give lip service to love. That's okay if we accept the challenge to change the way we think by backing up what we say. When we stand behind our words, we begin to establish faith and trust with those that we wish to have as friends.

Most of us project an image based on what society tells us is acceptable. We think about fancy cars, lots of clothes and jewelry and how much money and prestige we have. We usually try to live up to and protect this external image by conforming to what everyone else is doing. People want to be accepted so they follow behind one another instead of thinking for themselves. We cannot establish sincere friendships with a robotic mentality. We must have faith and think for ourselves.

You are what you think. It cannot be otherwise. Consider the friendships that you have established. You thought your friends into your life, and the friends you have thought you into their life. It is rude to invite people into your life only to mistreat them. We should treat friends with respect. If we cannot do this, it is because we are not treating ourselves with respect. We have not accepted the beauty of ourselves and we are attracting people who have not accepted their beauty or don't treat themselves with respect.

Most of us have conditions for friendship. When the conditions change, the friendship also changes. This is not what real friendship is supposed to be about.

Many of us like to talk about the friendships that we've maintained over a long period of time because rarely do people actually maintain their friendships. This is because true friendship allows everyone to learn and grow without conditions. In a judgmental society, unconditional friendship, like unconditional love, is difficult to accept.

All relationships can be based on friendship. Parents, children, mates and others can be seen as friends first. It simply requires a conscious decision to accept this approach.

With each experience, people learn and evolve. If you appreciate the people in your life, why not learn and evolve with them? When you can do it unconditionally and without judgment, you maintain the joy and pleasure that comes from true friendship.

There is a book titled *People Are Never The Problem* by Robert Watts Jr. In his book he asserts that people are not the problem, but that they have problems. With this premise, he offers a new paradigm for understanding ourselves as well as others. He states that to distinguish between *having* a problem as opposed to *being* the problem, helps us to more objectively look at what is happening in order to better address the issues. Once we personalize what the problems are we identify and attach ourselves to the problem. We will not be as inclined to establish a friendship with people who we see *as* the problem as opposed to people *having* a problem.

During the spring of 1990, I happened to be in court suing the landlord of the building I live in for one of the many reasons that had the two of us constantly in and out of court. While there, I met a woman who also happened to be in court dealing with a court case. She had a very friendly personality, and we hit it off immediately.

I had known her for about three months when she found out that the roommate I shared the space with was moving out. She asked me if she could move in when the room was available. I told her that if she did, we would have to stop dating. She agreed and moved in soon after.

Six months later, she mentioned that she couldn't believe it was possible to live in the same house with someone she had dated without that person approaching her for sex. She told me how much she respected that, and if the relationship were to remain platonic, she would like to become my adopted sister.

I was surprised and flattered. She asked me to discuss it with my grandmother and mother. I did and they accepted her. From that moment on, she became a member of the family.

As time went by, I marveled at her loyalty and trust in the relationship. At first, other women I knew found it difficult to believe that I would accept any woman as my sister. They would sometimes sleep over and wake up in the morning surprised to find that she was pleasant and friendly.

With some of my male friends, it was a different story. Most of them took it for granted that I was sleeping with her. When I'd tell them I was not, they became interested in going out with her. When they asked me if they could take her out, I would laugh and make it clear that they would have to ask *her*. She went out with many of them and seemed to have a good time.

At first, some would ask me how I could not approach her for sex, living under the same roof. I sometimes stopped to explain that she was very serious about whatever man she would take up with, which probably resulted from the fact that her parents had been married for 60 years. Her mother knew no other man in her entire life but her father. I'd explain that there was no way I would even consider playing with her feelings just for a moment of pleasure.

I remember explaining this to Robert Watts, Jr., when he mistook her for my wife. It was he who suggested that I include this information in the book. For me, this story demonstrates the ultimate in friendship. I have known many women who've expressed a desire to establish a friendship. However, it *seems* that whenever a romantic relationship did not work out, the friendship didn't work out with many of them. I would have loved to have had a true friendship with all of them.

I began to realize how the scarcity of mature and balanced men has created psychological pressure that has made most women more concerned about romance than friendship, despite what they say. They would like to be friends with whatever man they are interested in, but their focus is on romance instead of friendship. If women focused on friendship first and walked away from men they could not be friends with, there would be fewer broken hearted women and more lasting relationships.

Many women are disguising their true feelings as a result of dealing with selfish and unsympathetic men. This is not in their best interest because it continues to help women set themselves up to be hurt by the very same men they should be open and honest with. When you are open and honest with yourself, you will not accept destructive and negative behavior from someone else.

I don't think that men try to establish real friendships with women because there isn't any sincere and meaningful communication between them. Things that could be understood and dealt with are often overlooked and ignored. If we want to establish meaningful friendships, we must see things differently and start to communicate how we really think and feel. When we can do this, true friendship will exist.

Romance

A princess in distress saved by a knight in shining armor, Robin Hood coming to the aid of Maid Marian, Cinderella rescued by the Prince, King Arthur protecting Queen Gwinevere, and many more such romantic stories are just as popular today as they ever were. These romantic fantasies are fed into our consciousness at an early age. As children we watch cartoons with romantic storylines all the time. As we get older, the stories become more sophisticated but the basic concept remains the same.

Is it any wonder that we grow up to imitate the same kind of romantic situations that we have been subliminally taught to duplicate?

Romance is ideally a wonderful concept. However, it is the illusion of romance that most of us are acting out. The illusion of romance is like a mirage in the desert. Men who were dying of thirst in the desert have told stories of seeing an oasis that disappeared the moment they tried to reach it. The illusion of romance, like that mirage, also tends to disappear when we try to reach it because it is not enough to support a relationship. We are acting out an illusion because our romantic fantasies come from the movies, television, songs and novels. We try to create real life out of stories that were meant to entertain us.

These mass marketing romantic media stories to which we are constantly exposed are funny, silly, overly dramatic and unrealistic. Usually some weak plot creates a romantic meeting, an equally weak twist in the plot separates the couple, and another ridiculous twist brings them back together.

Too many men approach women with illusions of romance and women look for this approach because this is what we are taught. It's very difficult to duplicate romantic concepts like the actors that we see in the movies. We can't solve life's problems the way Clint Eastwood does. When the movie is over, we leave the theatre and step back into the real world. Yet we still find ourselves trying to live up to unrealistic images by approaching romance from the outside - in (the movies) instead of from the inside - out (ourselves).

Many of us tend to act out romantic situations that are created by the media without realizing exactly what we are doing or where the influence comes from. The information we are using is superficial, and the foundation upon which these romantic stories are based is fiction. A void is now created between reality and the romance we would like to have. Since people are the type of creatures that won't admit to not knowing, we use our alter ego and our sense of vanity in place of honesty and sincerity to fill that void. It is through this process of turning to our alter ego that men inflate most of what they say in the same manner that vanity makes women ready to listen to anything said about them that sounds good.

Women naturally understand that love is the answer to all things. It's therefore easy for them to believe that romantic compliments might turn into love. Many women set men up to romance them. They may do so by dressing provocatively, using body language and also making romantic statements in place of honest communication, hoping that love will be the end result.

This does not create a realistic way in which to get to know the person that you would like to have romance you. Sincere communication must replace the mass media approach.

If true feelings are not being revealed, we are not being sincere with our intent. If we want a relationship to work, we have to be willing to express ourselves honestly. If we are not being true to ourselves, we are not respecting ourselves and we will attract a partner who will not respect us. Quite often this disrespect results in one of the partners trying to control the relationship.

When the romance dies, couples consciously and unconsciously struggle to establish who is in control. We have been conditioned to believe that men should have control over women. Although women are dissatisfied with men trying to control them, some women continue to accept it whenever a man shows he is capable of satisfying their desire for love.

The fact is, over a period of time this society has become very matriarchal. Despite how it appears, women are in control of their relationships with men. The fact that unnecessary challenges come with trying to control a relationship is an indication that it is not the thing for either partner to do or accept.

Control is often assimilated into our character because parents who loved us had control issues. The only person you can control is yourself. However, the less control you have over yourself, the more control you try to exert over someone else. This only creates more drama because you have stepped outside of yourself to address the challenges you face.

When you try to control a mate, you appear more like an adversary than a partner. As a result of this attempt to control, you also create pressure and a loss of freedom for yourself as well. How often are you asked, "Where are you going, why are you going and who are you going with?" When these kinds of questions become a daily routine, how can you feel free or happy?

At the beginning of many relationships, women often do not express themselves sincerely because of their concern with first impressions or the man's feelings about them. Hanging on to everything a man says and does for fear of losing a potential mate is not the way to approach a new love interest. Eventually who you really are and how you really feel and think about things will become obvious.

If couples are to achieve unconditional love, they must be willing to sincerely express themselves. Until they do, they will attract the same insincerity they put out and both parties will never achieve balance or secure a meaningful relationship.

I think that many people realize that the romantic stories in the media are not leading to a true romance. However, women still rush into the arms of the person they think they want to be with for the wrong reasons when they are caught up in the illusion that the media creates. If a man says something that a woman doesn't like, she usually walks away and leaves him talking to himself. This is why in the beginning of a potential relationship many men focus on trying to impress women with the illusion of romance instead of honesty because most women would rather hear what sounds good.

Women might think about not placing so much emphasis on the first impression. Unless a guy is definitely not your type, give yourself some time to move past the first few experiences with him.

If women know how to listen to a statement they don't like and immediately dismiss the speaker on the basis of those first few words, why are women having so much difficulty finding the ideal mate? Obviously the ability to learn about someone requires more time. People have more depth than the few words that you hear to determine who they are.

Why not look past the media-oriented programming and be honest about yourself and ask the object of your affection to do the same? If there are things you don't like about you, challenge yourself to become the better you because you can only attract yourself.

As we approach romance from the outside - in, men attempt to sweep women off their feet with gifts and a sense of their importance. Women also look for men to impress them this way. Without knowing it, women help set themselves up to be let down.

Why do you think women scream, swoon and faint at music concerts that feature their favorite superstars? At these concerts, they are able to get a release from all of the romantic fantasies that are unfulfilled. They can also safely act out their romantic fantasies without the fear of being hurt.

The better approach to finding a real romance is to pay attention to how you naturally feel about someone. Why not take the time to see if you can appreciate that person you want to be with for who they naturally are? If the person that you are attracted to had nothing to offer you but themselves, would that be enough? Being anxious and rushing into a relationship usually doesn't work. Once a physical attraction is established, it alone cannot support a meaningful relationship because that's all it is, physical. If all you want is a physical relationship, that's your choice, but if you want more, the approach must be different.

Most people do want a meaningful and lasting relationship, but they have to be willing to challenge themselves and change their thinking in order to obtain this goal. They have to question the contradiction between what they really want and how they get caught up in popular notions of romance that have them trying to act out what they saw at the movies, read in a novel or heard in a song.

Religion

Why are people so ready to challenge each other for their religious beliefs? What is it about religion that does not allow people of different faiths to come together in the spirit of harmony?

Many of our ancestors believed that the Creator was in everybody, in everything and existed everywhere. They believed that the Creator was represented by the Sun, which they called the Sun of God. They knew the Sun God gave life to all that existed and that the Sun Rays were an electrical and magnetic charge to the body, mind and spirit. They believed that the Creator lived within them; therefore, they communicated with the Creator daily and often.

As a result of their beliefs, indigenous people understood natural law and moved in harmony with nature and the natural order of things.

They understood that the earth circling the Sun is the reason for everything being in a cycle. As a result of the earth circling the Sun, plants, insects, animals, mammals, humans, birds, fish and all living things deposit their seed to continuously duplicate life ad infinitum. They knew that the earth going around the Sun gave this third dimensional planet its seasons and its natural laws, especially the absolute law of cause and effect; for every action there's an equal and opposite (opposame) reaction. What goes around will always come back around.

Akhunaton is considered the most important Pharaoh of Egypt because he was the first Pharaoh in recorded history to practice the worship of one God. The Egyptians had begun to lose their belief in one God and one Spirit that moves through everything to worship many gods. Akhunaton reintroduced the Christ consciousness understanding of the Oneness of everything, with a new religious worship of the Sun, responsible for all life. Akhunaton possessed the occult knowledge that the Sun reflected every thought and every action (like a giant mirror) and that every thought and every action would be reflected right back. If you killed someone, you would be killed. If you cheated or stole from someone, someone would cheat and steal from you.

Thousands of years later, western civilization told indigenous people that they were pagans because of their belief, with a religion not worthy of civilized human beings. They taught the indigenous people they had conquered that the Creator was outside of everything, and that it was necessary to have a middleman such as a priest or rabbi in order to communicate with the Creator. They felt it was necessary to construct a building that represented religion in order for people to go inside to worship properly. Communication with the Creator was to take place once a week, presided over by the middleman within that building. Donations were accepted from the worshippers as a sign of good faith. These are just a few of the rules that the conquered people were told to follow.

We all watch movies. If we pay attention, we can learn a lot about ourselves. Consider the movies you've seen that centered on indigenous people. Consider further what those people were like before their religion was taken away from them. Now add to this how those same people turned out once they embraced someone else's religion.

At one point, indigenous people were full of life, with a freedom of thought that they themselves had nurtured, and they had a sense of self-definition. At another point, they became passive, afraid, vulnerable and insecure about themselves. Once they had accepted the belief from other people that God was outside of them, they lost their God consciousness and ultimately lost their natural sense of themselves.

Most of us agree that there is only one Creator. However, each one of us tends to claim, mold and shape the one Creator to fit one's own particular design. In effect, we join whatever religious group that appeals to the way we think about God. This multifaceted approach to the worship of God has caused many wars for thousands of years. Instead of religion bringing us closer together into one human family, we have separated ourselves without any signs of finding a solution that would move us closer toward the One Consciousness.

Eventually humanity will reach its highest consciousness. However, the road we are presently on makes the journey very painful and infinitely longer. We spend much of our energy and time attempting to achieve selfish goals while disregarding the spiritual and natural law that is necessary to create a proper balance between the spiritual and material.

People talk about a vengeful God, a God to be feared, and what group of people God did or did not curse. Why would God want to take vengeance on anyone, or have people living in fear, or curse any group of people? To do this would make God biased and small in stature. Humanity's destiny would then be pre-determined without free will and choice existing in order to balance our lives.

The vengefulness, the fear and the curses that have been attributed to God are negative ideas promoted by man. These beliefs keep us on a painful karmic road that leads to more pain until we change our thinking.

The biblical story of Eve and Adam clearly implies that if Eve had not bitten into the fruit, we all would still be living in Paradise. Yet there are people

221

who believe that Adam was responsible for humanity's eviction from The Garden. They say had Adam not listened to Eve and bitten into the fruit, we would still be in Eden. Some believe Eve was doing exactly what she was supposed to be doing—reflecting against Adam's manhood. In other words, all Adam had to do was remind Eve that they were not supposed to have eaten the fruit. Adam would have demonstrated his will power and Eve would have been happy and secure in the fact that she had a mate who acted responsibly.

To emphasize their point, it's said The Creator did not dismiss them from the garden until Adam had actually bitten into the fruit. If this is true, the eviction was a reflection upon Adam.

If the eviction was a reflection upon Adam, why is it that both Eve and Adam paid the price? The answer makes a statement about the collective happiness and suffering that women and men can experience, especially when the positive side of their oneness is understood, appreciated and lived.

In none of the widely recognized religions are women equal with men. Why is that? Religion has played a large part in the hardship that women have experienced throughout the centuries. Why is that? We are not discussing politics, we are not discussing business, and we are not discussing sports or the social hierarchy of someone's position in life. We are talking about religion and our worship of God!

The bible says that Eve was made from Adam's rib. Is this true? If it is, who was there to observe it? If no one was there, who channeled this information down through history and why? If female and male were once one being, is it possible that this one being separated itself exactly in half through its own level of consciousness in order to better appreciate learning from each other?

Why are we telling women that they cannot be equal in the eyes of God? What does that mean? And what does that say about men? Was this man's way of creating a form of slavery for women in order to have control over their vaginas? Are we so insecure with ourselves that we pull women down as a way to lift ourselves up? Man will only reach the lofty heights that true manhood represents when all issues regarding equality are addressed.

There is a religion called The Truth. It's been here all the time. The Truth allows us to understand the things that are, to give credit to The Creator who made things as they are, and to act accordingly. Nothing resonates like The Truth.

The Messenger or the Message

While technology has developed at an alarming rate, humanity has not been able to keep up with the pace. One of the ways humanity lags behind can be seen in the approach we take when making choices. We allow all kinds of personal reasons to keep us from making the right decision, especially regarding other people. Our decision-making process regarding others is influenced by the smallest reasons, from how we feel about somebody's taste in clothes to how we feel about a person's smile.

We cannot afford this superficial approach when trying to decide who may or may not become our mates. People are more than what the initial impression may imply. How often have you heard someone say, "At first, I didn't like her or him, but now we're the best of friends?"

How often have you seen a situation where two people couldn't stand each other, and six months later you receive an invitation to their wedding?

We must make our choices based on being able to see someone for the person they are instead of the person we would like them to be. It's not easy choosing correctly when we are not being objective and approaching our choices from a personal point of view. That's why it takes time to choose the right mate. Time allows the romantic high to wear off so we can come back down to better see things as they are.

Many people are attracted to each other because they accept the wrong message being delivered by the messenger. This false message is delivered in the form of a person's profession, how wealthy one is, how important one appears, how beautiful or handsome they are to look at, and a host of other messages that don't describe who the messenger is as a person. These are not the qualities upon which one can build a lasting relationship. The character, personality, sense of humor and degree of responsibility that the messenger manifests is the true basis for a lasting relationship.

We also cannot afford to indulge ourselves in superficial concepts when it comes to choosing things of a professional and progressive nature. I talked to a friend of mine about an herbalist I was taking classes with. The herbalist was excellent at what he did. I introduced them by phone. After talking with him, my friend didn't want to meet him. She didn't like what he said or the way he said it. I suggested she overlook the messenger and focus on his message. I told her how he had helped cure my mother, who had a serious case of sugar diabetes, with herbs and a change of diet. My mother's experience didn't make a difference to her. The messenger remained more important to her than the message.

The United States of America has a great deal to offer its people. As a nation of people striving to be the best that we can be, it is not in our best interests to disregard the valuable messages that the wealthiest country on the planet offers us because we have personalized our messengers. Why would any messenger be considered more important than the message? Today, if Paul Revere rode through the streets shouting that the British were coming, we would be more concerned about what kind of clothes he had on, who his parents were, whether or not he was handsome, tall, short, fat, small or smiling.

Everyone knows someone who gives advice or passes on information that they themselves may not be following. The normal response from a person who might be receiving this information is usually, "Why should I listen to you? You're not listening to yourself." This response does not diminish the importance of the message.

The message is like a concept, and a concept is the foundation that a system (of thinking/doing) is built upon. It's the same as a singer and a song. The song is the concept upon which the music and the singer are built. You can have a great singer, a great production and a great arrangement, but if the song does not measure up, you may only sell a handful of CD's. On the other hand, you can have a mediocre singer, a mediocre production and a mediocre arrangement, but if the song is a great one, you can sell a million CD's.

Everyone is aware that the United States is a melting pot for different nationalities from around the world. Have you noticed how many ethnic groups will protest injustices that only affect their group? It does not matter if the injustice is occurring in their mother country or within the United States. They will galvanize themselves into action. They will bring the family, and call up friends and everyone else who comes from the same country. We have been falsely programmed to believe that this approach is best.

The protestors represent the messenger. However, it's the message that they want to deliver that should take precedence over who is delivering it and to whom it is being delivered. Most messengers don't care about anyone else's message but their own because of racism and selfishness.

People of all nationalities should think about collectively coming together to deal with all-important messages. This is the method that will produce the best results. We know that there is strength in numbers. So why are we so ready to place emphasis and importance on the messenger?

They tell us that we live in the 21st Century. It's time to get off the horse and step into the spaceship. It happens mentally. The horse and the spaceship exist within our minds. A simple decision to collectively address any and every important message that affects humanity as a whole is the only way to be effective.

When I was first looking for investors for *The Children's Health Food Book*, I was involved in two negotiations that stood out. I had done business in the past with someone I considered a business associate and a friend. I showed him the completed manuscript and drawings, and he was impressed. Two days later, he faxed me a three-page agreement. As I read it, I stood in the middle of the floor for about 20 seconds with my mouth open. For $10,000 he wanted total control over the book and me. I passed on the deal but left the door open to do business with him in the future.

Two years after the book was printed, I received a call from someone that I had known for twelve years. I had not seen or heard from him in nine or ten years. He said that he had seen the book and was managing a major celebrity. He asked me if I was interested in worldwide distribution, getting on the Oprah Winfrey Show and selling a million copies. Without skipping a beat I said it depended on the deal. He came by my place the next day. We discussed what I considered to be a great deal for both of us. When I received the 17-page contract from his lawyer, it was as if we had never sat down to discuss the deal at all. This was yet another attempt for someone to take total control over another's work. I called him and said, "We agreed to agree but your lawyer is killing the deal."

He invited me over to his office. We sat down to discuss the deal again. After nine months and three different contracts, I told him I'd rather pass on the deal. When he realized that I was actually going to pass, he asked me what kind of deal I wanted. I told him that it didn't need to be on 17 pages. I explained that this was a simple deal that could be put on one page. He told me to get it done. I was able to get it on two pages. We signed it and I was finally thrilled with the plans to promote and market the book.

Just prior to printing the book, he and the celebrity parted ways. This killed our deal, because he would invest his money in ventures he thought would be profitable in collaboration with the celebrity who would promote and market the product. Without the celebrity in his corner, 50,000 books would be too risky a venture.

I cite the above examples because both of these gentlemen were good businessmen in spite of our failure to do business. I did not personalize the way they did business with me. It was business it wasn't personal. Their message, as good businessmen, was more important.

People represent energy. We should all focus on how to best share in each other's energy in order to move forward with the least resistance. Since we live in a world where economics takes precedence over most things, it becomes important that we use our energy to move each other forward in business. However, when you try to take advantage of me or I try to take advantage of you, the energy we both exert is negative. Negative energy creates negative results.

Money

"The love of money is the root of all evil."

Who said that? It must have been the same crew who told us that Eve came from one of Adam's ribs and was the one responsible for Adam's eating the fruit that got them both thrown out of the Garden. Certainly the way we use money to control other peoples lives makes it appear to be the root of all evil. It seems that our selfish desire to possess as much money as we can has made it the main purpose for having it. There are many people who could not possibly spend all of the money they have accumulated if they lived 100 lifetimes.

People seem to be fond of saying America is a great country. America is a wealthy country. There's a difference between being great and being wealthy. Imagine what kind of world we could create if America used its money to achieve the greatness attributed to it.

America must first start with being concerned about the people in its own country. We can not deny people employment and then lock them up for committing crimes without everyone paying a price for it. The same concern can be made about housing for the homeless and free health care for everyone.

Thomas Jefferson once said that we are all entitled to life, liberty and the pursuit of happiness. He should have said life, liberty and the pursuit of as much money as we can get because this seems to be the standard by which we live.

The material possessions we obtain when we have money seem to take precedence over the happiness we are all entitled to. What we want requires a constant flow of cash money in today's world. Consequently, most of us have laid aside our principles, our integrity, and our sense of humanity in the pursuit of the almighty dollar.

Many people believe that money is the only thing that will make them happy. Most of us have heard the statement "Be careful of what you ask for, you just might get it." This became a popular statement because, in many cases, what people wanted did not make them happy when they got it. Once the satisfaction of achieving what is desired wears off, people are still left with their fears and insecurities.

Some women have made a conscious decision to seek a mate based on the amount of money he has. Just as many men have made a conscious decision to attract a mate with their money. There are also women who use their money to attract a mate they want. This doesn't work because once the novelty of the money wears off, what's left is not enough to create the happiness desired. As a result of this, many relationships exist without love or affection. Many people believe the absence of love is the reason why we are destroying the planet and ourselves.

The potential to accumulate large sums of money in America is so great that many of us focus on nothing else. Of course, money makes a difference and can add to your happiness. But money does not make The Difference. If it did, there would not be so many unhappy people with lots of money.

We are born in a world that planted the seeds of selfishness into the culture of our society long before we arrived. Consequently, many of us have grown up thinking selfishly. We have a very selfish sense of self, and spread this selfishness while pronouncing how important we are and how much we want to help other people.

There are parents who look their grown children in the eyes and tell them how much they love them. Yet, these same children must ask their rich and wealthy parents for material things that they can't afford. These parents put their children and other loved ones in the will so they can inherit whatever they wish to leave them after they die. Why do your children and the people you love have to wait for you to die before they share in your wealth?

I believe this kind of thinking explains why wealthy people are not often loved by their relatives. Some of these relatives have murdered or attempted to murder their wealthy relatives in order to inherit the wealth sooner than later.

Waiting until you die before you share your wealth with those you love is an antiquated concept that came out of the Middle Ages. Noblemen, well past their prime and too old to rule were reluctant to pass the power to their first-born male children while they were still alive.

History is full of examples of assassinations that were attempted, and in many cases carried out, by the next in line to the wealth and power. Our lifestyle is not the same as it was in those feudal times. However, this outdated concept is still very much a part of our lives when it comes to money.

The titles, "Nobleman" and "Lord," had nothing to do with how noble or Godly someone was. It was an indication of wealth and power. It separated the rich from the poor. The poor were called peasants, and the name was indicative of having no rights. The noblemen and lords acquired their sense of self-importance and security through someone else's misery, poverty and pain.

In today's world, people who are wealthy and do not help to address the needs of others with their wealth are maintaining this obsolete and self-centered approach to life. Many people on the lower rungs of society that make more money or have more assets than their neighbors exemplify this same outdated mindset.

We are not feudal lords or knights controlling peasants and farmers as they did in the Middle Ages. We are not in constant battle over small plots of land or caught up in playing one feudal lord or knight against the other in order to secure and protect the power. Times have changed drastically and yet those feudal power struggles are still going on.

People are tired of the old paradigm of doing things. When enough people accept the principle of caring and sharing with others, we will reach the point where we will not be concerned about struggles to control anybody or anything.

Wealthy people, and in particular wealthy parents, should be willing to share their wealth with those they love and the less fortunate. You can't take it with you, and when you die you will not have had the privilege of spending or giving away your money.

There are two gentlemen I know who have put together two awesome but different business ideas that they were able to get off the ground. One obtained investors from two different sources but still needed money. The other was able to get as many professional people as he needed to invest their time and energy to help him with his project because he is well respected in his community. However, he had no money. Both of these gentlemen mentioned something during a meeting that blew my mind.

The one who got the investors has a father who is very wealthy but would not give his son any money toward his project, even though he knew the son was going to succeed and become very wealthy. The other gentleman's father refused to give him any money toward the project, even though he was on his deathbed, and intended to leave the son and daughter the wealth when he died.

Women understand living in the moment better than men do. This is why they also understand how to spend money now in order to enjoy the moment. Men would be wise to take this same approach. It's only paper!

The value that money has is the value that people have placed upon it. Money is only worth the paper it is printed on, and the paper is not worth very much. Originally, paper money was backed by gold deposited in a safe and secure place. The amount of money printed was supposed to be backed by the exact amount of gold deposited. Eventually, greed caused those in control to devalue the dollar and print as much paper as they wanted to, regardless of its original value or the actual amount of gold it was backed by. Unfortunately, this practice does not take into consideration all of the trees destroyed every year to print the money used.

Money is an illusion that we ourselves have created. Fear and greed have made this illusion our reality. We need to re-evaluate many of the outdated ideas that we have about money and realize that it is best used to create a better life for everyone.

There is nothing wrong with using money to attract a mate if giving and receiving love is the bottom line. There is nothing wrong with using money to attract a mate if sharing the wealth and spending the money is done unconditionally.

Music

How important is music?

Music is sound. And sound and light are just as significant as time and space. The significance of music is better appreciated when we are taught the effect it has on the body, mind and spirit.

There are people who believe that in the beginning there was light while others believe that in the beginning there was sound. Could it be possible that sound and light are one and the same? Is it possible that in another dimension, sound can be seen and light can be heard?

Whenever we are exhausted or depressed, most of us are able to change our emotional and physical state by playing music we enjoy. We have heard people talk about being so caught up in a particular form of music that they could feel it throughout their body. We

241

have all witnessed the involuntary movement of some part of the body when we hear music we enjoy. We have seen people automatically start to dance upon hearing certain music. We've also seen and felt the discomfort when not being able to dance or hear the music we like. These situations are indicative of how important music is.

In 1987 a friend, Tico, and I were taking music theory classes once a week from Artie.Sheppard. At our very first class, Artie had both of us hum a sound. He said whatever sound each of us hummed was our natural sound. Thereafter, whenever we had a class, he would start us out humming our particular natural sound as we practiced going up and down the scales.

He explained to us that everyone had a natural sound, and if we learned to approach music from the point of our natural sound, it would make music easier to learn as opposed to everyone starting with 'C' Natural, which is the way music is taught.

At the time we were learning this approach, I thought it made sense, but I didn't think much more about it. As I now remember the experience, it takes on a much greater significance in terms of understanding the inward self. Our personal sound is just as important as our astrological sign. I believe that every sign in the zodiac has a corresponding sound that is natural to that sign. If this information were taught in the school system, these classes would help students to understand and appreciate how unique we all are.

It has also been researched and documented that colors (the colors in a room, the colors we wear and the colors we see) have a healing affect on the body, mind, emotion and spirit of a person. Research may discover (if it hasn't already) that color, light and sound together can have unlimited possibilities in healing the human body of disease.

Children should be given music classes for at least the first five years of school. They can then decide if they would like to continue taking classes. I have never heard of anyone not enjoying some kind of music.

The healing effect of music may sound like magic, but it works naturally. During the slave period in the Americas, Africans proved that singing made a difference in how they felt working and how much they were able to accomplish in spite of the impossible work load and harsh conditions. This is traceable to the work songs of communal Africans and convicts in the fields and other work details during and after slavery.

Chain gangs throughout the south were more effective when African prisoners sang songs as they worked on the roads. Whenever prison guards didn't allow singing, there would be a noticeable decline in how much road was actually finished.

Most of us are aware that the sound appreciated by one person might not appeal to someone else. There are those who like low sounds while others appreciate high sounds. I don't believe that this is just a coincidence.

Is it possible that being female or male plays a part in what type of sounds we naturally like? Could time of birth, parents, or where we were raised, be factors that determine what sounds appeal to each of us?

I am not talking about the type of music we like. We know that what type of music we like is definitely influenced by what we grew up listening to. I'm referring to pure sound, which is any sound that may not be part of a melody, like a yell, a single note, a cough, a car crash, and so on.

Experiment and use your imagination. If you have a baby, watch how the baby reacts when you do and don't play music. You might try the same thing on your pet, if you have one. Experiment with different kinds of music.

Couples might experiment with each other, especially if there is anxiety in their relationship. Focus on playing music that is calming and soothing. Keep a journal to record the time, the day and the reaction. At the end of four to six months, the journal should reveal extensive information about your respective attitudes with and without music.

When the science of music has been fully researched and made available to the public, we will be able to scientifically verify what we already know in our hearts; music enriches our lives and fosters better relationships.

The Problem With Women Is Men

Hip-Hop

The art form known as hip-hop has moved across national and international markets like a cultural tidal wave. It has infused everything in its wake with economic, social and political empowerment. hip-hop has also captured the heart and imagination of young people around the world.

Today's hip-hop culture is reminiscent of yesterday's bebop phenomenon. Like bebop, hip-hop is a subculture that is also defined by the music, language, and fashion.

Once bebop was created, it drew followers who began to personalize the music. When personalizing anything you imply that it is something that is exclusively created for you. Most bebop musicians saw it as an ethnic phenomenon that others should not be privy to. They viewed it as a sort of private club for them and for a select group of hip white musicians who had proven themselves. Many of the musicians also looked down on other forms of music and refused to play or acknowledge any other music except bebop. However, the more enlightened creators like Charlie Parker, Dizzy Gillespie, Miles Davis and Thelonius Monk understood that all forms of music should be listened to and appreciated. It was years before the majority of other bebop musicians accepted this message.

Many bebop musicians played by ear because they had not learned to read music. Most of them were from low-income families and used music as a way to make ends meet and possibly obtain fame and fortune. They also used heroin and other drugs to escape the pressures from an unsympathetic society. A subculture was created based on the common lifestyle these musicians shared. This lifestyle made it easy to personalize the music that they helped create.

When a creative genius like Charlie Parker used heroin, thousands of other musicians and music enthusiast followed in his footsteps. Many of them believed that if they used heroin, they would become great musicians like Bird, or get to be accepted by the "hip crowd." Famous artists like Miles Davis, Dexter Gordon, Fats Navarro, and other great artists the public never got a chance to appreciate because they could not overcome the drug habit, personalized what they believed bebop to be, and suffered because of it.

The creators, artists and followers of hip-hop, as with bebop, have done much to personalize this art form. The creators of hip-hop have taken it, shaped it and interpreted it in terms of what it means to them as opposed to what it means unto itself. When you personalize your point of view to the extent that you can't see objectively, you create the possibility that the end result can become negative. Hence the manner in which the males treat the females.

The personalizing of hip-hop by many of its creators has also manifested itself in the way it is used to describe and justify the kind of lifestyle which most of these artists live. Since the majority of these artists also come from inner cities and low-income families, their experiences have been similar. Their social condition is the basis for a common lifestyle and attitude. Thus, the stories that they rap about are very similar, and many of those stories are negative. The myth they have created dictates that women are "bitches," men are "niggas," and taking someone's life for something done or not done is the rule not the exception. In the early stages of the hip-hop phenomenon, partying and having fun was the standard. It then evolved and became more socially conscious and political in nature. It was at that point when major producers and artists became more inclined towards what is referred to as gangsta rap.

If the message exemplifies negative and destructive behavior, that's how the messenger will be perceived.

Several of the hip-hop artists and producers that I have known and worked with over the years don't really approve of these negative messages, but most of them have not changed their lyrics because that is what sells.

Many of them now have families and are concerned about the children listening to the negative messages in hip-hop. They don't consider themselves "niggas" or the wives or mates "bitches," and they realize the negative affect these messages are having on today's youth. However, they want to be famous and wealthy, so they just perpetuate the cycle, knowing the potential havoc it is causing. Fortunately enlightened artists are beginning to realize that the negative messages in hip-hop need to change and are taking steps to do it.

In the world of hip-hop, women are acting and dressing like men in order to achieve equality with men and to be accepted into the subculture. The polarity that exists between men and women is getting wider as hip-hop grows. These same men and women may well be each other's future mates. Without realizing it, they have been setting the relationships up to fail. Women are not going to accept being treated like "bitches," and men are not going to accept women disrespecting them for the "niggas" they are made out to be. Famous artists who deliver these messages are not living like that. Yet, the young people who listen to hip-hop are trying to live the messages in the music.

Women will automatically lose respect for men who cannot come up with a workable answer to everyday problems. The illusions coming out of hip-hop offer few answers. As men become less responsible

251

because they have no answers, women become more aggressive and manly because the hip-hop lifestyle is intense and aggressive.

It's a natural progression of life that as men get weaker, women get stronger. Women are already naturally strong, but their strength is internal. It manifests externally whenever men don't back up what they say. At such times women will argue, fight and challenge men in the same manner that men challenge each other. Women who refuse to become aggressive will still not respect men that don't act responsibly. Meanwhile, many men will believe that it's the woman's fault because she doesn't understand.

There's a much larger world out there than the neighborhoods or cities urban youth grow up in. In that world, they are not respected, in part because of the messages they give as representing hip-hop. What's worse is that urban youth are feared as well as disrespected. The hip-hop generation is also giving birth to children who are following in their footsteps to be feared and *further* disrespected because of the image that Hip-Hop projects.

How many times can the problem be stated without supplying some answers?

hip-hop is like the sleeping giant that rocks itself to sleep, a giant that has created its own pacifier and insists on keeping that pacifier in its mouth as a form of rebellion.

What appears to be rebellion is more like self-destruction. bebop was the same way, in that the artists rebelled against themselves. It was a different day, but the same game: creative geniuses tripping on the edge of self-destruction.

How many of us genuinely understand how great Charlie Parker or Billie Holiday was? Too many of us only got to see glimpses of their greatness because it was concealed by their own self-destructive behavior. Their greatness, as working artists, and their genius, as individuals capable of achieving great things, was never fully realized.

Yesterday's geniuses allowed themselves to be stepped on. Today's celebrities are held in higher esteem and have greater influence over old and young alike. Thus, the new breed of celebrity is solicited and paid to represent and promote everything, from status quo politics and causes to cheap products and false ideas. It becomes very easy for them to disregard the fact that their message is negative because they are being well paid. The public has put too much importance on the celebrity who now acts as the messenger.

When celebrities gain fame from an art form, it is important that they draw the line to determine what they should and should not represent. This can help to offset the self-destructive lifestyles that so many people get caught in.

Why shouldn't hip-hop assimilate and dispense information and knowledge that will help people learn to become better human beings? In the process of appreciating art that comes with negative information, many people assimilate the information and it becomes a part of what they do and how they live. With this approach we help to slow down our evolution into productive human beings.

There are answers to all of the destructive messages in hip-hop that people need to hear from its creators. The social problems that are reflected in hip-hop lyrics are real, but the lyrics do not provide practical answers. What's the point? Aren't rappers artists? Shouldn't art be about education and beauty as well as problems and tragedy? John Oliver Kilens, the novelist said, "the responsibility of the artist is not only to tell it like it is, but to also tell it like it ought to be."

Suicide

Since pre-recorded history, people have been taking their own lives for one reason or another. The reasons are many and varied, and the impulse to do it takes but an instant to fulfill.

In some cultures, a warrior would actually take his life if he felt he was responsible for a battle being lost. In some nomadic tribes, the very old or very sick would go off to die if they believed they were endangering the lives of the group by not being able to maintain the speed of the group. Martyrs throughout history have accepted death over giving up their ideas about life. Today, the people we now call terrorists give their lives for a cause they believe to be greater than themselves; their people's state of oppression.

What I find mind-boggling is the large number of young people in The United States who have committed or tried to commit suicide. Since young people are the future of every country, you would think that every country, especially the wealthiest country in the world, would be more concerned about the future of their young people.

As a nation of people, we have not created the balance between the spiritual and the material worlds, so we remain out of balance. This lack of balance between the spiritual and material has created mass confusion that has resulted in people, particularly young people, committing suicide. Without balance nothing will work.

According to The Center for Disease Control, over 500,000 young people in the United States attempt to end their lives each year, and over 5,000 actually succeed in killing themselves. It has also been said by experts who study death that 5,000 suicides a year would double if what we call "accidental deaths" (drug overdose, drowning, automobile crashes) were recognized for what they are – other forms of suicide.

According to research, suicide is the ninth leading cause of death in the U.S. There are more suicides than homicides, and suicide is the third leading cause of death among teenagers.

When the students of Columbine High School shot and killed other students in that now-famous massacre, not only were they taking the lives of other people, they were also sentencing themselves to death.

Parents must pay more attention when children begin to give hints about taking their lives or wishing that they were never born. The general consensus among adults seems to indicate that suicide is not a major issue in the lives of young people. Yet, that does not alter the fact that far too many young people think about, attempt to take or actually take their own lives.

According to the researchers who have questioned failed suicides, people have said that they can't take the pressure anymore because the pain, stress and confusion is too much for them to deal with.

Pain, stress and confusion often result in some kind of serious drug abuse. Since alcohol is a legal drug, there are more alcoholics than there are drug abusers of other types. When we view the two categories as one, the statistics verify that (a) drug users are more prone to commit suicide than anyone else; and

(b) alcohol is the number one drug responsible for suicide.

According to statistics, females make more attempts to end their lives, but males are three times more likely to complete the act.[6] Men are more likely to shoot or hang themselves while women are more likely to overdose on pills or slash their wrists. Pills and wrist slashing afford an opportunity for the victim to be rescued or to reconsider the attempt. There is no opportunity to reconsider a gun or a rope.

Why are more females attempting suicide than males? What part does an unfulfilled relationship play in females attempting to take their lives? Could it be that women are more susceptible to the pitfalls of low self-esteem and adversity when it comes to relationships? Are the challenges of life greater and harder for women than men?

I had a female friend who used to get angry when I said that men have the capacity to make women happy. Her position was that people make themselves

---

[6] Healthier You: Ask the Mental Health Expert Archives 2001-2004, Male *vs* Female Suicide

happy. If this is true, why are so many women's states of unhappiness traceable to the men in their lives?

In a holistic universe, how can you be happy with only half of yourself? Sure you can learn to love half of yourself, but that only helps to keep you from being totally unhappy. It doesn't make you happy; it only makes you less unhappy. It's like making love without being in love. You can receive a degree of physical gratification, but it won't touch your soul or brighten your spirit.

Emperor Nero of Rome once tried an experiment to test the power of love. He instructed twenty nursemaids not to speak to or show any love or affection toward the twenty newborn babies in their charge. Within one year every single baby died.

Babies are the most recent arrivals through the Universe into this world. Like women, they are also more vulnerable to any disharmony and lack of affection they may experience. The fact that every single baby died indicates how necessary love and affection are to the human experience. We must become more responsible and improve the conditions in which we live by moving with the lightness of being instead of the heaviness of the drama. When we can do this, we will be better able to appreciate life, and fewer suicides will occur.

We can not continue to deny people jobs and condemn them for stealing, withhold medical insurance and watch people die, or spend billions to cure diseases that are caused by the use of manmade chemicals. There is no logic associated with this approach to our survival. When people begin to get a sense of all the destructive practices we perpetrate upon ourselves, it becomes easy to understand why some people might want to leave the planet sooner than later.

Women represent a gauge through which to understand how close or how far away we are from a level of stability necessary for love and happiness. Attempts at suicide especially by women indicate that there are still serious challenges that we all need to address.

Whales, like people, are intelligent mammals. When groups of whales deliberately beach themselves, I believe they are committing suicide. It seems to me that they are telling us how unhealthy it is to live in the environment humans have created.

In order to help prevent suicides, we must begin to research the causes and provide some answers. The sum can never be greater than the source. People are the source of everything that happens in life, positive and negative. There is nothing too big or too small that comes out of us that we cannot understand or overcome. It's all a part of our personal learning experience.

If the road we are on is leading us into actually committing suicide, obviously we need to get off that road and take another one. We don't have to get stuck or attached to anybody, thing or idea, especially when it is leading us to self-destruct.

We must become explorers of our personal world. If what we find is not enhancing our lives, we must move into other arenas and continue the exploration with an open and unattached mindset. When our minds are open and we don't attach ourselves, we are able to learn from the experience and continue to move forward. The people we meet and associate with enable us to see exactly what kind of journey we're on. Whatever and whoever we attract is based on how we think and what we want out of life.

There are spiritual laws that guide us. When we have learned these spiritual laws that help us on our journey, we can accept and understand what is meant by reincarnation. When the principle of life and its never-ending cycle is better understood, we can each see that committing suicide disrupts the journey. When we return again, we come right back to that same position in life we were at before the suicide.

Suicide can be compared to a straight line. When the line is broken, cut or interrupted, life momentarily stops. When the line is reconnected, each individual life continues from that same particular point at which the line was broken. Thus, whatever pain or pressure we once tried to escape from is still a part of life when we are born again. Why not bite the bullet and go through whatever the challenge is in the present. Why would anybody want to repeat the same painful lessons? It's the same as getting left back in school and repeating the class. Imagine getting left back hundreds of lifetimes to go through the same pain again and again and again.

When we learn to live without judgment and embrace love in an unconditional manner, we move further away from the depression that makes us want to commit suicide. When we accept each other as equals, we take the first major step towards creating peace within ourselves because we learn to see ourselves in each other. This sincere acceptance will not allow us to create pain for ourselves, for anyone, and not for anything.

The Problem With Women Is Men

Epilogue

Throughout the years I have been asked by women and men to teach them the knowledge that I have acquired over time, concerning the pressing issues of life. As a student myself, in the classroom of life, I have come to realize that any "knowledge" that I have or anyone has for that matter, is from a universal body of greater wisdom and understanding. There is nothing that anyone can teach to others because we all have the knowledge within us. We just have to be reminded of what we have forgotten. As such, what we really need is a cultivation and reintroduction to those faculties that connect us to universal consciousness.

First of all, we need to realize that we are in a matrix so diabolical that it makes the movie "The Matrix" seem like a comedy. The matrix in which we live is so much worse than the movie because in the movie humans defeated the machines. However, unlike machines, we cannot defeat ourselves. We wind up inflicting serious pain upon ourselves first, and that's exactly what we are doing, living life through pain. We are like an organism feeding off of itself instead of feeding itself. How can anything survive feeding on itself?

In order to step out of the matrix that we live in and step into the real world, we need to change the way we think about things. We will not be able to do this unless we understand that everything is in a circle – the planet, our cells, our thoughts, everything.

When you look into a mirror, you see yourself. When the mirror is removed, everything you see in front of you is still you. It is not possible to see anything else but yourself. When you believe that the things you see in front of you are separate from who you are, you help keep yourself stuck in the matrix. Russell Simmon's book "Do You" is appropriately titled.

We also remain stuck in the matrix because we think in a straight line. Linear thinking does not allow people to understand anything. It creates illusions that appear real. This false reality dictates that we see life from other people's point of view. If we are told that the world is flat, we accept it and believe if we sail too far out into the ocean we will fall off the earth. We also fight to stay in the matrix by taking offense against those whose opinions and lifestyles do not agree with ours.

Although men act and women react, when you understand that everything is in a circle, you will know that reincarnation is a part of life's cycle. You will also accept that the sexes are interchangeable, men come back as women and women come back as men. Whether you come back as a woman or a man, you will eventually learn whatever the lesson is so that you can evolve to become the greater you.

The actions of men have brought heavy drama to the playing field of life. Women have reacted with the same degree of drama hoping that men get the message and make life better. In order for men to measure up to their potential, there is one step that must be taken first. A man must keep his word when he gives it. If a man cannot keep his word, he maintains his desire to think in a straight line wondering why things don't work right.

As a woman, you can also do your part to create the happiness that you seek. To do this you must stop being concerned about how you think a man feels about you and focus on how a man is going to treat you. This is just as important to you as a man keeping his word. Feelings change from moment to moment. Feelings are so elusive that they can't even be discussed intelligently with a potential mate. However, you can intelligently discuss how a man intends to treat you and how you would like to be treated.

When I was in college I wrote and copywrited a song called "Men" that is consistent with the message in this book. As time passed, I became more convinced that men would not be able to find their way out of the darkness because of their selfish nature.

About 25 years ago I said to a close female friend, "I am going to start an organization of women." She asked "What about the men?" In spite of my plans to do otherwise, I realized that she was right. This book is my attempt to do justice to that understanding.

"Surviving the Matrix."   Due September 2010

My name is Ron Seaborn and I have a message for men. The price that I have paid to bring you this message is as intense as the message that I bring. I chose to accept this challenge because I wanted to address what I saw going on around me. "The Problem with Women is Men" was written so that it could be used as a tool to better help you understand the story and message in "Surviving the Matrix."

The level of destruction that we have created can be gauged by the way women treat children. How intense is the treatment? They are abusing children in the name of love as a result of how they feel about themselves

Drugs, sex and money are the corner stones of what I have seen motivating a large percentage of women because they are not being properly motivated by men. When the foundation that stimulates their response to men is drugs, sex and money instead of love – lies, half truths, and selfishness become tools that women use to protect themselves and at the same time act aggressively toward men and each other.

This is a story stranger than fiction and unbelievably true.

INDEX